DALIT VISIO~

Gail Omvedt is a sch~
movements, especia~
organizations. A Ph.D fro~
been a citizen of India sinc~ ~volved
in anti-caste campaigns sin~ ~nic writings
include several books and ~ ~~, caste and gender
issues, most recently *Reinventi~ ~lution: New Social Movements
in India* (1993) and *Dalits and the Democratic Revolution* (1994). She is
a consulting sociologist on gender, environment and rural
development and lives in Kasegaon in southern Maharashtra.

TRACTS FOR THE TIMES / 8

Dalit Visions

The anti-caste movement and the construction of an Indian identity

(Revised edition)

GAIL OMVEDT

Orient Longman

DALIT VISIONS

ORIENT LONGMAN PRIVATE LIMITED

Registered Office
3-6-752 Himayatnagar, Hyderabad 500 029 (A.P.), INDIA
e-mail : hyd2_orlongco@sancharnet.in

Other Offices
Bangalore, Bhopal, Bhubaneshwar, Chennai, Ernakulam, Guwahati,
Hyderabad, Jaipur, Kolkata, Lucknow, Mumbai, New Delhi, Patna

© Orient Longman Private Limited 1995, 2006
First published 1995
Reprinted 1996
This revisied edition 2006

ISBN 81 250 2895 1

Typeset by
Scribe Consultants
New Delhi

Printed in India at
Sai Printo Pack Pvt. Ltd.
New Delhi

Published by
Orient Longman Private Limited
1/24 Asaf Ali Road
New Delhi 110 002
e-mail : olldel@del6.vsnl.net.in

Contents

Preface

This tract deals with the way in which the Dalit movement and other social forces have confronted and contested brahmanic Hinduism not only its most virulent form of *Hindutva*, but equally the more liberal forms that have provided the dominant interpretation of Indian society and history. It does not deal, except in passing, with the economic and material base of the "Hindu" construction and the challenges to it. What are the economic foundations of caste and religion? What were the material forces that allowed brahmanic Hinduism to gain hegemony in the Indian subcontinent, that allowed "Hinduism" to be constructed as it was during the colonial period, that allowed Congress rule to be consolidated? What are the material and economic forces today that make *Hindutva* so virulent and powerful? And on what material basis and with what political forces can it be fought?

While these are all important questions that will have to be answered, they do not come within the purview of this particular tract. The symbolic and cultural sphere, whether we consider it to be "secondary" to the material base or of equal weight, has a logic of its own. This is true even if it is seen as interwoven and interacting with economic and political forces. Indian leftists have not paid adequate attention to cultural and symbolic issues. They have thus not confronted the meaning and forms of the brahmanic hegemonizing of Indian culture. This has been done by the dalit/anti-caste movement and to some extent the other social movements of the recent decades. The time has now come to learn from this history of contesting Hinduism.

In destroying the Babri Masjid on December 6, 1992, the forces of *Hindutva* issued a declaration of caste war, not simply an assault against the Muslim community. The act and the statements surrounding it made it clear that the VHP, Shiv Sena and sections of the BJP were not prepared to respect the decisions of the courts or the laws of the land regarding the "birthplace of Lord Ram" and that the "Dharma Sansad" was being posed as higher than the people's parliament. This was a declaration of war against dalits, adivasis, women, the bahujan samaj, the toiling and productive castes and classes who have always been held as inferior by *varnashrama dharma*. That war has to be fought, at the level of culture and symbolism and not simply that of politics and economics; and not simply with the weapons of "secularism" but over every inch of the terrain of Indian history and identity that the Hindu-nationalists have staked a claim to.

The imposition of brahmanic dominance on Indian culture has produced "Hinduism"; the fight against this has been as long and old as the story of that imposition. This tract represents a survey of some of the important moments of that fight.

Editorial Preface

TRACTS FOR THE TIMES will attempt to provide meaningful information, critical perspectives, and theoretical reflections on various themes of contemporary concern. The tracts will seek to deepen our knowledge of crucial issues, query our commonsense, re-think old concepts, and analyse the social and economic problems we confront.

This tract explores and critiques the sensibility which equates Indian tradition with Hinduism, and Hinduism with Brahmanism; which considers the Vedas as the foundational texts of Indian culture, and discovers within the Aryan heritage the essence of Indian civilization. It shows that even secular minds remain imprisoned within this Brahmanical vision, and the language of secular discourse is often steeped in a Hindu ethos. The tract sets out to look at alternative traditions nurtured within dalit movements, which have questioned this way of looking at Indian society and its history. It seeks to understand the varied dalit visions which have sought to alter the terms of the dominant order.

Omvedt shows how different phases of the dalit movement opened up new ways of looking at the structures of their oppression and the premises of their emancipation. Jotiba Phule saw the caste system as the essence of Hinduism and sought to unmask the culture of oppression that it sustained, the brutal slavery that it sanctified. In his reinterpretation of the Aryan theory, the Aryans emerge as cruel and violent invaders who subjugated an egalitarian society and imposed a hierarchical and exploitative system with Hinduism as its legitimating ideology. Tarabai Shinde and Pandita Ramabai unravelled another layer of cultural subjugation. Characterizing Hinduism as patriarchal ideology, they questioned the traditional morals embodied in Brahmanical texts, seeing them as the basis of women's oppression and patriarchal domination. By the 1920s anti caste and anti Brahman movements acquired a more popular basis. Some of them asserted a dalit identity within terms set by Brahmanical Hinduism: fighting for Kshatriya status and the right to enter temples. Others — like the Ad Dharm in Punjab, Adi Hindu movement in Hyderabad, Adi Dravida in Andhra and Adi Karnataka in South India — traced the history of their oppression to Aryan conquest and claimed that the non-Brahmans were the original inhabitants of these different regions. Influenced by Marxism, Ambedkar sought to build a unity of dalits and non-Brahman middle castes which would be both a class and caste unity against the brahman-bourgeois Congress. When Hindu communalists emphasized the link between blood, territory and language and projected Hindi and Sanskrit as the quintessential Indian languages, other linguistic groups reacted in the same mould, and identified themselves as separate nations. The centralizing tendencies within Hinduism and nationalism produced a reaction: movements against caste and Brahmanism became revolts of the regions against north Indian domination. The 1970s saw a new turmoil, the emergence of a new radicalism. The Dalit Panthers attempted to project the proletarian essence of dalit experience, and explore the inner connection between cultural and economic struggles.

Omvedt's argument moves at two levels. At one, she discusses the different phases of the dalit movement, their visions and ideals, their understanding of the link between religion, culture and power, between caste, gender, and class oppression, between language and identity. At another level, Omvedt develops her own perspective on dalit emancipation. In the dialogues with different dalit visions, one can hear the authorial voice. Omvedt appreciates efforts to forge a unity between sudras (backward-castes) and ati-sudras (untouchables): separate and independent movements of these groups are seen as self-debilitating — the basis of their weakness and failure. She criticizes those who divide the issues of economic exploitation and cultural oppression, and the issues of class and caste; and she endorses the attempts to transcend these separations.

Omvedt's conception of Dalit as a category may appear problematic to many. It emphasizes the congruence of interests between the backward castes and untouchables where others may prefer to see conflict and opposition; it focuses on the affinity in the experiences of these groups where others may underscore the fact of difference. But this tract will force us to reconsider our ideas, to question assumptions and categories which we take for granted, and to re-examine our conception of history. It will persuade us to listen to those voices which we often refuse to hear, and understand those visions which have sought to change the world in which dalits live.

NEELADRI BHATTACHARYA

1

Introduction

For most people, even scholars, "Hinduism" has been a taken-for-granted concept. Hindus are the people of India. Hinduism is their religion. Beginning with the Rg Veda to the philosophers and even contemporary political leaders, it has been seen as a unique phenomenon of spirituality linked to a practical life; and with a solid geographical base in a diversified subcontinent. Although its stability has been broken from time to time by invasions, conquests and disturbances, it has nevertheless maintained a fair continuity. It has given birth to rampant and unjustifiable social inequalities but has also spawned the protests against these. Its greatest virtue has been its elasticity, its pluralism, its lack of dogma. Hinduism, it is said, has no 'orthodoxy' (though it may have an 'orthopraxy'). With a core in the religious tradition going back to the Vedas and Upanishads, it has brought forth other sister/child religions—Jainism, Buddhism, Sikhism—all born out of the same fertile continuate of tradition, all part of India and Hinduism's contributions to the world.

This image, encompassing the cultural diversities of the subcontinent and subordinating them to a Vedantic core, has pervaded both popular and scholarly writings on India. To take but one example, two scholars of "religion in

1

Maharashtra" draw together dalit, Marxist and *bhakti* traditions in a book entitled *The Experience of Hinduism*, only to give Vedantam the last word:

> Buddhists, Jains, Muslims, Christians, nay even the Marxists, of today's India cannot help partaking of it—they are all Hindu-Bharatiya at heart.... What is it to be a Hindu-Bharatiya? What does it involve? Chiefly, the accepting of the other world as well as this world, the attempt to reconcile the two. But between the two the other world comes first. *Brahman* and *maya* are both real, but brahman is the ultimate reality.... This ultimate/provisional duality has been resolved into a unity in the Vedanta of nonduality.[1]

There are many, as this tract will demonstrate who would contest this violently. What is more striking, though, is that behind the image of flexibility and diversity is a hard core of an assertion of dominance. "Between the two the other world comes first". This assertion leads to the political line of the Vishwa Hindu Parishad that there may be various versions of what is defined as the "Hindu tradition" (Sikhism, Buddhism, Jainism, Arya Samaj and Sanatan dharma are the ones usually mentioned), but there is no question that the core is "traditional" Hinduism—*sanatan dharma*.

Out of the pleasantries of the official ideology of Hindu pluralism and tolerance and under the pressures of contemporary material deprivation and economic turbulence, has grown the modern politics of *Hindutva*—militant Hinduism, Hinduism as nationalism. It makes a simple addition to the claim that Hinduism is the main religion of the people of India: Hinduism is the national religion, the people's tradition in the subcontinent, but it has been attacked, smothered, insulted, dishonoured, first by Muslim aggressors, then by British colonialism, and now by the contemporary State which in its self-definition as "secular" is dishonouring it in

its own land and pampering Muslim and Christian minorities. Hinduism's great virtue was its generous tolerance of
other faiths, but its enemies have taken advantage of this;
Hindus must now be strong, fierce and proud, and not hesit-
ate to assert themselves.

Today, large sections of left and democratic forces and all
new social movements are trying to argue and organize
against the growing influence of *Hindutva* or Hindu-nation-
alism. The majority of these have taken a position against
"communalism" but not against "Hinduism" as such. The
"secular" version of this opposition argues that Indians must
come together beyond their religious identities, as citizens of
a nation and as human beings. It is exemplified in the popular anti-communal song *Mandir-Masjid*:

> In temples, mosques, gurudwaras
> God is divided.
> Divide the earth, divide the sea,
> But don't divide humanity.
> The Hindu says, 'The temple is mine,
> The temple is my home.'
> The Muslim says, 'Mecca is mine,
> Mecca is my loyalty.'
> The two fight, fight and die,
> Get finished off in fighting...

The song goes on to describe the machinations of political
leaders and the perpetuation of exploitation through communalism, but interestingly enough, even its appeal to a
common identity draws on (and reproduces?) the notion that
India is the home of the Hindus while the Muslims find their
loyalties elsewhere.

Another mode of opposing communalism is to re-appeal
to Hindu traditions themselves, a position that has been developing among several anti-communal Delhi intellectuals
over the last few years. This has been eloquently voiced by

Madhu Kishwar in a number of *Manushi* articles which argue "in defence of our dharma". Agreeing with the condemnation that Nehruvian and modern left secularism are insufficient to deal with the need for identity, she appeals to *bhakti* traditions as the "true Hinduism", and argues that the militaristic image of Rama is a distortion, and that much of casteism is in fact a colonial heritage. This position has antagonized many secular feminists, but there is no denying that it is persuasive to many, particularly to middle class, upper-caste Indians. Even the upper-caste left is being increasingly drawn to it. This is illustrated by the poster of the Sampradayikta Virodhi Abhyan: the mask of Rama, the form of Ravana. The SVM thus appeals to the "gentle" image of Rama and takes for granted the demonical quality of Ravana.

These two forms of opposition to Hindutva, the "secular" and "Hindu reformist" versions, draw respectively upon Nehruvian and Gandhian traditions. While there is no reason to doubt the genuineness of their attempts to oppose the aggressive politics of the Hindutva forces, one can question the validity of their picture of Hinduism: the validity of the general identification of "Hindu" with "Bharatiya", of Hinduism with the tradition of India.

Beyond this debate between the secularists and the Hindu reformists there are many voices in India today which not only query the BJP/VHP interpretation of Hinduism, but also contest the very existence of Hinduism as a primordial force in India. A Tamil dalit scholar-activist, Guna, writes:

> The very concept of Hinduism, which took shape in the north only when the Muslim rule was being consolidated ... was never known to the Tamils until the period of British colonization.... The Brahmans, who had English education and had the opportunity of studying abroad, took some threads from the Europeans who conceived of a political entity called

4

'Hindustan'. With the borrowed idea, they could clumsily merge the divergent cults and Brahmanic caste apartheid to term it as Hinduism. This concept ... resulted in formulating a pseudo-religious-political concept called 'Hinduism', based on which they sought to define their myth of a 'Hindu' nation-hood.... The 'Hindu' was thus born just two centuries back; and he is still a colourless, odourless and form-less illusory artificial construction.[2]

Guna is part of a broader tradition or set of traditions which have put forth alternative interpretations of Indian identity(or identities). These have been socially based among the lower castes, dalits and non-Brahmans, drawing on peas-ant (and women's) traditions, mainly in the southern, west-ern and outlying regions of the subcontinent. In contemporary times they draw on such leaders as Phule, Ambedkar, Periyar; they appeal to heroes of revolt such as Birsa Munda and Veer Narayan Singh; they claim the tradi-tions of Buddha and Carvak, Mahavir, Kabir and Guru Nanak and Basavappa; they claim heroes like Shivaji but contest the Hinduist interpretation of him; they claim the glories of Mohenjo-daro and the heritage of the pre-state tribals as opposed to that of plundering Aryan tribes. In con-trast to the secularist opposition to Hindutva they proclaim a politics of identity, and in contrast to reformist Hindu iden-tities *they define 'Hinduism' itself as an oppressive class/caste/pat-riarchal force.*

The dalit movement, based on ex-untouchables and widening to include non-brahman castes of many southern and peripheral areas, has in recent times brought forward most strongly this ideological challenge, this contesting of Hinduism. Indeed the impetus to challenge the hegemony and validity of Hinduism is part of the very logic of dalit politics.

5

It is insufficient to see dalit politics as simply the challenge posed by militant organizations such as the Dalit Panthers, the factionalized Republican Party, the rallies of the Bahujan Samaj Party, or even the insurgenciés carried out by low-caste based Naxalite organizations. Dalit politics as the challenge to brahman hegemony took on wider forms throughout the 1970s and 1980s, its themes sweeping into movements of "backward castes" (the former shudras of the traditional varna system), peasants, women, and tribals. Dalit politics in the sense of a challenge to brahmanic tradition has been an aspect of "several new social movements." Strikingly, if we take 1972, the year of the founding of the Dalit Panthers, as a beginning year for the new phase of the dalit movement, it was also a crucial year for many other new social movements—from the founding of SEWA in Ahmedabad to the upsurge of a new environmental movement in the Tehri-Garhwal Himalayan foothills, from the agitations and organizations of farmers in Punjab and Tamil Nadu to the rise of tribal-based movements for autonomy in the central Indian region of Jharkhand. These movements though not as directly as the dalit movement, came to contest the way in which the Hindu-nationalist forces sought to depict and hegemonize Indian culture. They often linked a cultural critique to a broader critique of socio-economic development and an opposition to the over-centralized political system. By the late 1980s, an intermixing and dialogue of all these themes could be seen. The events of 1989-1991 ended with a setback resulting in the renewed aggressiveness of the forces of Hindu nationalism, but we continue to hope that the setback has been temporary.

2

The Construction of Hinduism

Is "Hinduism" only a construction, and a recent one at that? In a sense all nationalisms and identities are constructions. It also seems accurate to say that the identification of the Indian subcontinent with a single people whose religion is Hinduism was only made in recent history, and only in recent decades has it been projected as a national religion centring on Rama.

The term *Hindu* is ancient, deriving from Sindhu, the river Indus. The Hindu religion as it is described today is said to have its roots in the Vedas, the poems of the Indo-Europeans whose incursions into the subcontinent took place many centuries after the earliest urban civilization in India. Most archaeologists today doubt that the "Aryans" were the main force responsible for the destruction of this civilization, but it seems fairly clear that many of their early poems celebrated its downfall, with the rain god Indra claiming to be the "destroyer of cities" and the "releaser of waters." In any case, whatever we call the religion of these nomadic clans, it was not the religion that is today known as Hinduism. This began to be formulated only in the period of the founding of the Magadha-Mauryan state, in the period ranging from the Upanishads and the formation of Vedantic thought to the consolidation of the social order represented by the Manusmriti. Buddhism and Jainism (as well as the materialist Carvak tradition) were equally old, and Jainism's claim tracing its heritage back to Mohenjo-daro has some validity. Hinduism, as we know it, was in other words, only one of many consolidations within a diverse subcontinental cultural tradition, and attained social and political hegemony only during the sixth to tenth century A.D., often after violent confrontations with Buddhism and Jainism.

It was in this period that the subcontinent as a territory came to be known throughout the world as Hindustan. But this did not refer to religion and the Muslim rulers of the land were also known as Hindustanis. The major strands within what was later to be called Hinduism were known separately in the south as Shaivism and Vaishnavism, and their influence spread throughout southeast Asia as separate traditions.

The main themes of brahmanic Hinduism, the identification of orthodoxy with acceptance of the authority of the Vedas and the brahmans, along with a tremendous absorptive and cooptive power as long as dissident elements accepted their place within a caste hierarchy, can be seen from this period. The material base of this social order lay in the village productive system of caste, *jajmani* and untouchability. Nevertheless it is doubtful whether the masses of the people at this time identified themselves as Hindus. There were numerous local gods and goddesses who remain the centre of popular religious life even today; and the period gave birth to bhakti or devotional cults (sometimes centred on non-Vedic gods such as Vithoba in Maharashtra) which rebelled against caste heirarchy and brahman domination. Many of these in turn developed into religious traditions that consider themselves explicitly non-Hindu (Sikhism, Veerasaivism).

It was, in fact, only the colonial period which saw a consolidation of the identification of India or Hindustan (the land) and the people who inhabited it, with a particular religion known as Hinduism, interpreted as being the primal and ancient religion of the subcontinent. This was the construction of Hinduism. The Europeans, with their racism, romanticism, fascination with the Vedas and Orientalism, played an important role in this. But the major work of constructing Hinduism was done by Indian elites. In the nineteenth century, people like Lokmanya Tilak adopted the "Aryan theory of race", claimed a white racial stock for upper-caste Indians and accepted the Vedas as their core literature. Tilak was also the first to try and unite a large section of the masses around brahmanical leadership, with the public celebration of the Ganesh festival. Anti-Muslim themes underlay the construction of Shivaji as the founder of a "Hindu raj," a process, incidentally which was ideologically contested even in the nineteenth century.[1] By the end of the century, Hindu conservatives were mounting a full-scale attack on their upper caste reformist rivals with charges that the latter were "anti-national," and succeeded in excluding the Social Reform Conference from any coordinated meetings with the National Congress.

Significant developments took place in the 1920s with the founding of the Rashtriya Swayamsevak Sangh (RSS) by Hegdewar and the Hindu Mahasabha by Savarkar. Savarkar was the first to proclaim a full-scale Hindu nationalism or Hindutva, linking race, blood and territory. He proclaimed himself an atheist and his theory laid less emphasis on religion as such; yet his Sanskritic, Aryan interpretation was clear: he disliked any idea of mixing Hindi and Urdu, refused to admit the linguistic/cultural diversity of India, and was consistently anti-Muslim in his politics.

Tilak and Savarkar were Maharashtrian Chitpavan brahmans, the caste which comprised rulers displaced from power in western India by the British. The Chitpavans were already under pressure from a strong non-brahman and dalit movement by the 1920s. Significantly, the claim to an Aryan racial heritage was given a major reinterpretation in the 1930s, clearly under pressure from the non-brahman movement's reversal of it: Aryanism and the notion of a Vedic, Sanskritic core to Hinduism was not given up, but it began to be argued by ideologues like Golwalkar that the Aryans themselves had had their original home in the Indian subcontinent.[2]

Nevertheless, Hindu nationalism found its strongest base in north India, the only place where the emotive slogan "Hindi-Hindu-Hindustan" made sense. Here, the previous empire had been controlled by Muslims and there were still large numbers of Muslims of all social sections. Thus, beneath the ideological formulation of 'Hinduism as nationalism' was a growing identification with religious community. Peasants, artisans and others identified themselves in religious terms, with "Hindu" and "Muslim" communities emerging as independent entities out of what had been a fairly deep linguistic-cultural synthesis, in a process which Gyan Pandey has described as "the construction of communalism in north India." Both groups not only formulated their identities in religious terms but called for political power to protect them. As Pandey describes the process, "the idea of a Hindu raj which would reflect the glories of the ancient Hindu civilization and keep Muslims in their place" was "matched in due course by the notion of a Muslim Raj which would protect the place of the Muslims."[3] These tensions gradually led to efforts at organizing an identity at the national level.

Once it was accepted that two separate communities, Hindus and Muslims, existed at an all-India level, there were only two possible courses for creating an overriding national identity. One was taken by Gandhi, the other by Nehru and the leftists. The Gandhian solution involved taking India as a coalition of communities, each maintaining its identity but uniting by unfolding the wealth of tolerance and love which lay in each religious tradition; the Nehruvian solution consisted of forging a secular identity on the basis of modernity and socialism that transcended, and in the process rejected, separate religious communal identities.

Gandhi's solution rested on a deep recognition of the importance of popular traditions; indeed throughout most of his political life his ability to draw upon such traditions helped make him the most important mass leader of his time and in formulating an ideal of development that was different from the centralized industrial path later followed. Gandhi identified himself as a Hindu, but gave his own, sometimes breathtaking, interpretations of what it meant to be a Hindu. "The *Vedas, Upanishads, Smritis* and *Puranas* including the Ramayana and the Mahabharata are Hindu scriptures," he notes, but then insists on his right to interpret. He rejects anything that does not fit his idea of spirituality: "Nothing can be accepted as the word of God which cannot be tested by reason or be capable of being spontaneously experienced."[4] But inevitably this very acceptance of the Hindu identity meant an absorbing of the caste element of this identity:

Caste has nothing to do with religion ... it is harmful to both spiritual and natural growth. *Varna* and *Ashrama* are institutions which have nothing to do with castes. The law of *Varna* teaches us that we have each one of us to earn our bread by following the ancestral calling... The calling of a Brahman—a spiritual teacher—and of a scavenger are equal and their due performance carries equal merit before God and at one time seems to have carried identical reward before man.[5]

This was a formulation that accepted a hereditary place or calling for a human being and would obviously be rejected by militant low castes.

Gandhi's social reformism as well as his proposed

11

developmental path, a kind of 'green' projection of a sustainable, decentralized society that grew out of a powerful critique of industrial society, were in the end tied to a Hinduism that accepted a brahmanic core: the limitations of needs in which both technology and sexuality were seen as tying humans down to desire (*maya*), and in which the guiding role of intellectuals was accepted. '*Ram raj*' made Gandhi ultimately not simply a Hindu but also an indirect spokesman for upper-caste interests.

Not surprisingly, Gandhi had his biggest aspirations, confrontations, and failures on the issue of caste. Gandhi's clash with Ambedkar at the time of the second Round Table Conference showed that he put his identity as a Hindu before that as a national leader.[6] Many of the lower castes were in the end alienated from Gandhi's version of anti-communal Hinduism, notwithstanding his courage, or his murder at the hands of militant Hinduism itself. Ambedkar's judgement—"this Gandhi age is the dark age of Indian politics. It is an age in which people instead of looking for their ideals in the future are returning to antiquity"[7]—was harsh, but expressed the dalit choice of modernity over the Hindu version of tradition.

But the other alternative, Nehruvian secularism, had its own problems. Like Gandhi, Nehru took the existence of a Hindu identity for granted. In contrast to Gandhi, his idea of building a modern India was to ignore religious identity, seeing it as ultimately irrelevant or of secondary importance in the modern world. Leftists and Nehruvian socialists alike took class as the ultimate reality at the social level, and sought to transcend this with an abstract nationalism, seeing all communal/religious identities as feudal. They believed that economic and technological development would make such identities redundant. Nehru's (and the left's) secularism thus seems indissoluble from a naive faith in industrial/scientific progress:

In my opinion, a real solution will only come when economic issues, affecting all religious groups and cutting across communal boundaries, arise.... I am afraid I cannot get excited over this communal issue, important as it is temporarily. It is after all a side issue, and it can have no real importance in the larger scheme of things.[8]

Nehru's secularism, as much as Gandhi's self-professed Hinduism, was underpinned by Hinduist assumptions about Indian society and history although he expressed, throughout his writings, a full appreciation of plurality and diversity. He says again and again that India is not to be identified with Hinduism, that Buddhism is a separate religion, that caste is to be condemned. And yet the broad framework of his thinking saw brahmanic Hinduism as the "national" religion, setting the framework within which other traditions could be absorbed:

Previously, in the ages since the Aryans had come down to what they called Aryavarta or Bharatvarsha, the problem that faced India was to produce a synthesis between this new race and culture and the old race and civilization of the land. To that the mind of India devoted itself and it produced an enduring solution built on the strong foundations of a joint Indo-Aryan culture. Other foreign elements came and were absorbed... That mixture of religion and philosophy, history and tradition, custom and social structure, which in its wide fold included almost every aspect of India and which might be called Brahmanism or (to use a later word) Hinduism, became the symbol of nationalism. It was indeed a national religion, with its appeal to all those deep instincts, racial and cultural, which form the basis everywhere of nationalism today.[9]

13

This had disturbing elements in common with the Hindutva discourse. Along with this, while Nehru condemned caste wholeheartedly, he disliked to see any intrusion of it into politics; he thought that demands (such as reservations) raised by non-brahman and dalit groups were divisive, and tried to ignore them. His historical discussion of caste sees it as essentially functionalist and integrative; it is clear that whatever the superficial influence of Marxism, his view of Indian society did not genuinely encompass a sense of exploitation and contradiction:

> Thus caste was a group system based on services and functions. It was meant to be an all-inclusive order without any common dogma and allowing the fullest latitude to each group.... The organization of society being, generally speaking, competitive and nonacquisitive, these divisions into castes did not make as much difference as they might otherwise have done. The Brahmin at the top, proud of his intellect and learning and respected by others, seldom had much in the way of worldly possessions...

Merchants, he argues, had no high standing, the vast majority of the population were agriculturalists with rights to the land who gave only a sixth share to the king or state: "Thus in a sense, every group from the state to the scavenger was a shareholder in the produce."[10]

Nehru's secularism then, shows the degree to which the "construction of Hinduism" in the late nineteenth and early twentieth century had succeeded in making a brahmanical interpretation of Indian social history hegemonic, not only for those who militantly identified as Hindus but for those who prided themselves on avoiding such an identification. In refusing to give legitimacy to the challenge of the anti-caste radicals, in ignoring the actual meaning of such constructions as "Hindu culture", the Indian left and

14

progressive elites allowed the maintenance of brahmanic assumptions of superiority and authority, the right of the elites to rule, and to assume the role of guardians. Nehruvian assumptions which saw communal harmony or "secularism" as achieved from above by a powerful state fit in easily with the statism that was to mark India's version of industrial development. As Pandey puts it,

> By the 1930s and 1940s, the importance of an 'enlightened' leadership was thus being stressed on all sides as the critical ingredient that was required in the bid to advance the 'backward' peoples... It had taken great leaders, a Chandragupta Maurya, an Ashoka, an Akbar, to actualize the dreams of Indian unity in the past and they had done so in the great states and empires that they had established. It would take great leaders like Nehru and Patel to realize the newly created unity of India, and the state would again be their major instrument. The twentieth century liberal ... could do no better than to turn to statism.[11]

What the "construction of Hinduism" successfully accomplished was to establish Hinduism as a taken-for-granted religion of the "majority" linked to the backward peasant core of a pre-industrial society. In this context Gandhi identified with it, and with the peasantry as he understood it; Nehru saw both as backward and inferior. Both accepted the brahmanic core of Hinduism and the need for a paternalistic enlightened leadership. Both responses ultimately failed; failed in overcoming a "Hindu" identity, in reforming it sufficiently to allow a full participation in its religious centre by the low castes, in preventing the growth of a virulent and aggressive form of the religion, interpreting it as the national identity of India. By the 1990s both Gandhism and Nehruism were reeling under the blows of popular disillusionment and the rise of the most virulent forms of "Hindu nationalism".

Right from the outset, though, a more fundamental challenge to Hinduism was taking shape. Its earliest major protagonist was a shudra (peasant) caste social radical from western India, Jotiba Phule.

3

Hinduism as Brahman Exploitation: Jotiba Phule

The extreme fertility of the soil of India, its rich productions, the proverbial wealth of the people, and the other innumerable gifts which this favourable land enjoys, and which have more recently tempted the cupidity of the Western Nations, attracted the Aryans.... The original inhabitants with whom these earth-born gods, the Brahmans, fought, were not inappropriately termed Rakshasas, that is the protectors of the land. The incredible and foolish legends regarding their form and shape are no doubt mere chimeras, the fact being that these people were of superior stature and hardy make.... The cruelties which the European settlers practised on the American Indians on their first settlement in the new world had certainly their parallel in India in the advent of the Aryans and their subjugation of the aborigines.... This, in short, is the history of Brahman domination in India. They originally settled on the banks of the Ganges whence they spread gradually over the whole of India. In order, however, to keep a better hold on the people they devised that weird system of mythology, the

17

ordination of caste, and the code of crude and inhuman laws to which we can find no parallel among the other nations.[1]

Phule's *Gulamgiri*, written in Marathi but with an English introduction, was published in 1885, the year of the founding of the Indian National Congress, but before the full-scale upsurge of Hindu nationalism, also before that principal proponent of radical nationalism, Bal Gangadhar Tilak, had become identified with social orthodoxy. The Brahmans whom Phule attacked so strongly were very often 'moderates,' liberals and reformers, grouped in organizations such as the Prarthana Samaj, Brahma Samaj, Sarvajanik Sabha and Congress. All of these were seen by him as elite efforts, designed to deceive the masses and establish upper-caste hegemony. Caste was to him *slavery*, as vicious and brutal as the enslavement of the Africans in the United States, but based in India not only on open conquest and subordination but also on deception and religious illusion. This deception was the essence of what the high castes called "Hinduism".

Jotiba Phule (1826-1890) was himself not a dalit, but a man of what would today be described as an "affluent OBC" caste, the Malis, gardeners by traditional occupation and classed with the Maratha-Kunbis as people of middle status. While he developed a strong dalit following, his main organizational work was in fact among the middle-to-low non-brahman castes of Maharashtra, traditionally classed as *shudras* and known till today as the *bahujan samaj*. He began as a social reformer establishing schools for both girls and untouchable boys, and founded the Satyashodhak Samaj in 1875, which organized the non-Brahmans to propound rationality, the giving up of brahman priests for rituals and the education of children (both boys and girls). His major writings include plays, poems and polemical works—poems attacking brahmanism, a ballad on Shivaji, and three books:

Gulamgiri which mainly focuses on caste; *Shetkaryaca Asud*, describing the oppression of the peasants; and *Sarvajanik Satya Dharm*, an effort to outline anew, theistic and egalitarian religion.

At the theoretical level too, Phule sought to unite the *shudras* (non-brahmans) and *atishudras* (dalits). He argued that the latter were not only more oppressed but had been downgraded because of their earlier heroism in fighting brahman domination. More importantly, he argued that shudras and atishudras together represented an oppressed and exploited mass, and compared their subordination with that of the native Indians in the Americas and the Blacks. Phule's broadsides are, in fact, an expression of a theory not simply of religious domination and conquest, but of exploitation.

The Aryan race theory, the dominant explanation of caste and Indian society in his time, provided the framework for his theory. This had been made the centre of discourse by the European "Orientalists" who saw the Vedas as an ancient spiritual link between Europeans and Indians, by the British administrators and census takers who classified the society they ruled, and by the Indian elite, people like Tilak who used it to justify brahman superiority. Phule turned it on its head, in a way somewhat akin to Marx standing Hegelian dialectics on its head, to formulate a theory of contradiction and exploitation: brahmans were indeed descended from conquering Indo-Europeans, but far from being superior, they were cruel and violent invaders who had overturned an originally prosperous and egalitarian society, using every kind of deceit and violence to do so, forging a mythology which was worse than all others since it was in principle based on inequality and forbade the conquered masses from even studying its texts.

By inverting the traditional Aryan theory, Phule took his critique of brahmanism and caste to a mass level. He used it to radically reinterpret puranic mythology, seeing the various *avatars* of Vishnu as stages in the conquest of India, while taking the *rakshasas* as heroes of the people. Central to this interpretation was the figure of Bali Raja. In Phule's refiguration of the myth, Bali Raja was the original king of Maharashtra, reigning over an ideal state of beneficence, castelessness and prosperity, with the popular gods of the regions (Khandoba, Jotiba, Naikba, etc.) depicted as his officials. The puranic myth in which the brahman boy Waman asks three boons of Bali and then steps on his chest to send him down to hell is taken by Phule as a story of deception and conquest by the invading Aryans. This reinterpretation had a strong resonance with popular culture, for in Maharashtra (as in other parts of south India, particularly Kerala) Bali is indeed seen as a popular and "peasant" king, and is remembered with the Marathi saying, *ida pida javo, Balica rajya yevo* ("let troubles and sorrows go and the kingdom of Bali come"). Similarly, the popular religious festivals of the rural areas are fairs centring around non-Vedic gods, all of whom (except the most widely known, Vithoba) continue to have non-brahman priests. Phule's alternative mythology woven around Bali Raja, could evoke an image of a peasant community, and his anti-Vedic, anti-Aryan and anti-caste equalitarian message with its use of poetry, dialogue, and drama, could reach beyond the literate elite to a wider audience of non-brahmans.

Phule's was not simply a focus on ideology and culture; he stressed equally the factors of violence and conquest in history (those which Marx had relegated to the realm of "primitive accumulation of capital") and took the peasant community as his centre. Violence and force were overriding realities in all historical processes; the "Aryan conquest" was simply the first of a series of invasions and conquests of the subcontinent, the Muslim and the British being the other major ones. It was, if anything, worse than the others not for racial reasons but for the fact that the "Irani Arya-bhats" solidified their power using a hierarchical and inequalitarian religious ideology. Brahman rule, or *bhatshahi*, was a regime that used state power and religious hegemony to maintain exploitation. The key exploited class/group was the peasantry, the key exploiters the bureaucracy which the brahmans dominated even under colonial rule. Taxes, cesses and state takeover of peasant lands were the crucial mechanisms of extracting surplus, supplemented by moneylending and extortion for religious programmes. Phule's graphic descriptions of peasant poverty, his sensitivity to issues of drought and land use and to what would today be called watershed development, and his condemnation of the forest bureaucracy make him strikingly modern in many ways.

Phule's theory can be looked at as a kind of incipient historical materialism in which economic exploitation and cultural dominance are interwoven. In contrast to a class theory, communities become the basis for contradiction (the shudra-atishudra peasantry versus the brahman bureaucracy and religious order); in contrast to changing property relations, conquest, force, state power and ideology are seen as driving factors.

Phule is today taken as a founding figure in Maharashtra not simply by the anti-caste but also by the farmers', women's and rural-based environmental movements. Apropos women, his personal life stands in contrast to the compromises made by almost every other social reformer and radical: he not only educated his wife, Savitribai and encouraged her to become a teacher in a school for girls, but also resolutely withstood all community pressures to take a second wife in spite of their childlessness. His writings assimiliated women into his general theories of conquest and violence (seeing them as the primary victims of force and violence, emphasizing the miserable life of peasant women). However, in his later years and under the influence of the

21

great feminist radicals of his day such as Pandita Ramabai and Tarabai Shinde, he took a stronger position describing male patriarchal power as a specific form of exploitation. The "double standard" which oppressed women was prevalent, he argued, not only as seen in the pitiable conditions of Brahman widows, but also in the patriarchy of shudra households in which the woman was expected to remain a loyal *pativrata* while the man was free to have as many women as he wanted.

Like all major dalits and spokesmen for the low-castes, Phule felt the need to establish a religious alternative, and his last major book, *Sarvajanik Satya Dharma*, details a noble-minded equalitarian theism, which also projects a strong male-female equality. In contrast to a secularism which assumes a Hindu majority and ignores all the problems associated with it, Phule attacked Hinduism at every point, challenging its legitimacy and questioning its existence. What is striking in his works is his refusal to even recognize "Hinduism" as such: to him it is not a legitimate religion but superstition, a bag of tricks, a weapon of domination. Thus he can refer in *Sarvajanik Satya Dharma* to the ideal family in which the father becomes a Buddhist, the mother a Christian, the daughter a Muslim, and the son a Satyadharmist—no scope for a "Hindu".[2] He never treats brahmans as simply a racial category, a group which is unalterably evil; but to be accepted they would have to give up their claim to a religion which makes them "earth-gods":

> When all the Arya-bhat Brahmans throw away their bogus scriptures and begin to behave towards all human beings in the way of Truth, then there is no doubt that all women and men will bow down reverently before the Creator of all and pray for the welfare of the Aryas.[3]

Analyses of Phule's thought are only beginning. He

22

wrote almost entirely in Marathi and in his time was little known outside Maharashtra. For a long time the lack of a communication network among low castes and the revulsion for his writings felt by most of the brahman elite made his work inaccessible. Even dalits often ignored him ("the problem with Phule is that he has no caste behind him," as one non-brahman radical activist commented) and although Ambedkar acknowledged him as one of his "gurus", very little of Phules's influence is actually seen in Ambedkar's writings. The Phule-Ambedkar centenary year (November 1990 marked Phule's death centenary and April 1991 Ambedkar's birth centenary), however, saw an upsurge of interest throughout India. Recently, the feminist scholar Uma Chakravarti has described Phule as a forerunner elaborating the theory of "brahmanical patriarchy",[4] while in a centenary year seminar organized by the Centre for Social Studies at Surat, G.P. Deshpande argued "that Phule was the first Indian system builder" providing a "logic of history," as Hegel did in Europe:

> Phule's thought proved that socio-political struggles of the Indian people could generate universal criterion. Phule also talked about knowledge and power much before Foucault did. In fact, Foucault's postmodernist analysis comes at a time when Europe has literally seen the 'end of history' whereas Phule's efforts were to change the world/society with the weapon of knowledge.[5]

Phule's argument that knowledge, education and science were weapons of advance for the exploited masses, was in contrast to all elitist theories that sought to link western science and eastern morals and argue that Indians could maintain their (brahmanical) traditions while adopting science and technology from the west for material development. For Phule, rather, *vidya* or knowledge was in direct contrast with the brahmanic, ritualistic *shastra* and was a weapon for equality and human freedom as well as economic advance. He constantly stressed the need for shudras and ati-shudras to stand forth and think on their own, and his response to the ideological confusions of his day sounds strikingly "post-modern":

All ideologies have decayed,
no one views comprehensively.
What is trivial, what is great
cannot be understood.
Philosophies fill the market,
gods have become a cacophony;
to the enticements of desire
people fall prey.
All, everywhere it has decayed;
truth and untruth cannot be assayed;
this is how people have become one
everywhere.
There is a cacophony of opinions,
no one heeds another;
each one thinks the opinion
he has found is great.
Pride in untruth
dooms them to destruction —
so the wise people say,
        seek truth.[6]

4

Hinduism as Patriarchy:
Ramabai, Tarabai and Others

Due to the efforts of Pandita Ramabai there was a beginning of education for girls and many great learned Arya Brahmans began to educate their helpless ignorant women to redress the errors of their rishi ancestors, but there may be many negative results of our critical writing about the tyrannical statements of the merciless Aryan bookwriters on women. Mainly this: fearing that when the cruel wickedness of the Aryan books come to the attention of the daughters and bhat-brahmans they will make mincemeat of all the legends of the temples and gods and mockingly reject them, and that besides, in most Brahman families a continual quarrel between mothers-in-law and daughters-in-law will arise and cause numerous tensions, many bhat-bhikshuks will stop sending their daughters and daughters-in-law to school and naturally will not give them even so much a glimpse of our *Satsar* book.[1]

Phule wrote this in a pamphlet in 1885 in response to attacks on two women, Tarabai Shinde and Pandita Ramabai. In 1882 Ramabai had come to Pune, founded the

Arya Mahila Samaj and then, shortly after, departed for England where she converted to Christianity. For this, she was condemned by even the moderate brahmans who had originally sponsored her efforts. Tarabai, a daughter of one of Phule's Maratha colleagues in the Satyashodhak Samaj, had written a bitter and hard-hitting attack on Hindu patriarchy, *Stri-Purush Tulna* ("Comparison of Women and Men") in 1882. Both women evoked waves of reaction, Ramabai in the wider world of the English-educated brahman intellectuals, Tarabai in Phule's own Satyashodhak circles; and Phule defended both.[2]

Pandita Ramabai was by far the better known of the two women and, in spite of her conversion to Christianity, accepted much of the framework of the brahman intellectuals of the time. She called her organization (undoubtedly the first autonomous women's organization in India) the Arya Mahila Samaj and focused her main English book on "the high-caste Hindu woman". She also continued to retain many brahmanic habits, in particular vegetarianism, as a symbol of her Indian identity—perhaps a necessary symbol for her in the face of often racist church pressure—and accepted the identification of "India" with "Hindu" and the Aryan model justification for caste hierarchy, arguing that the complete dependence and ignorance of women had been the cause of "the present degradation of the Hindu nation."[3]

> Without doubt, 'caste' originated in the economic division of labour. The talented and most intelligent portion of the Aryan Hindus became, as was natural, the governing body of the entire race.[4]

In spite of this and for all the frequent mildness of her language, it was Pandita Ramabai who was the first to proclaim, with great clarity, backed by her personal refusal to remain a Hindu, that the Sanskritic core of Hinduism was irrevocably and essentially anti-woman:

26

Those who diligently and impartially read Sanskrit literature in the original, cannot fail to recognize the law-giver Manu as one of those hundreds who have done their best to make women hateful beings in the world's eye... I can say honestly and truthfully, that I have never read any sacred book in Sanskrit literature without meeting this kind of hateful sentiment about women.[5]

Thus her conversion testimony stressed that there were

... only two things on which all those books, the Dharma Shastras, the sacred epics, the Puranas and the modern poets, the popular preachers of the present day and orthodox high-caste men, were agreed: that women of high and low caste as a class, were bad, very bad, worse than demons, as unholy as untruth, and that they could not get Moksha as men [could].[6]

In other words, in spite of her initial acceptance of most of the assumptions of Hindu nationalism, when it came to her own experience, this daughter of a wandering and reformist brahman, the only woman of her time to have been educated in the sacred language, who had fought her way forward to be recognized by the intellectuals of her time, had come to condemn the core of Hinduism as fundamentally patriarchal.

Harsher than Ramabai's writings were those of Tarabai Shinde. We know little of her life and virtually nothing of what happened to her after she wrote her book. It is clear that she did not go on to achieve the autonomy she so clearly strove for, and whether she ever managed to carve out even a small space for herself in the confined world of the nineteenth century Maratha landholding elite is something we shall perhaps never know. (Such spaces did exist, but were

27

available to very few.) *Stri-Purush Tulna* is her sole known testament, and the sound of a voice not-so-far-heard is its beginning:

> Since this is my first effort at writing, being helpless, bound and without a voice in the prisonhouse of the endless Maratha customs, this essay has extremely harsh language. But seeing that the new terrible examples of men's arrogance and one-sided morality that appear every day are ignored and all blame is put on women, my mind has been filled with the pride of women's position and gone into utmost turmoil.[7]

Tarabai was referring to the debate on widows who were blamed for trying to dispose their babies, the implications of sexual assaults on them being ignored. She was concerned about more than just atrocities; she attacked the whole pattern of life laid out for women.

> What is *stri dharma*? Endless devotion to a single husband, behaving according to his whims. Even if he beats her, curses her, keeps a prostitute, drinks, robs the treasury, takes bribes, when he returns home she should worship him as a god, as if Krishna Maharaj himself had come from stealing the milk of the Gavalis... There are a million reasons for breaking *pativrata*.

And she went on from this to a scornful, satirical attack on the gods and rishis of the puranas themselves:

> Now, even with five husbands didn't Draupadi have to worry about Karna Maharaj's intentions?... [What about Satyavati and Kunti?] One agreed to the whims of a rishi in order to remove the bad odour from her body, the other obeyed a mantra! What wonderful gods! What wonderful rishis![8]

28

Stri Purush Tulna takes the form of a diffuse and bitter polemic. It is not a reasoned, direct critique of the Hindu scriptures based on conceptual analysis, but a satirical attack on them in a language of familiarity. This was in fact the way in which many working class and peasant women talked about the stories they were so familiar with. The Ramayana and the Mahabharata were a part of the lives of the majority but this did not necessarily make them part of a religion, as was made out by religious spokesmen. When Hindu theorists began to turn such texts into "scriptures", women like Tarabai and Ramabai had to attack and reject them. Ramabai tried to create a different institutional framework with different human relations, and spent a lifetime in the service of high (and low) caste widows, whose position represented the most dire fate of women at the time. Tarabai, who was not in a position to do as much, expressed her rebellion in a bitter rhetorical attack on the structures of patriarchy:

> It was a woman, Savitri, who went to the court of Yama in order to save the life of her husband. But leave aside Yama's court, have you heard of any men who have gone even a step on the path towards it? Just as a woman loses her auspiciousness and so has to bury her face like a convict and live all her life in darkness, do you have to shave your beard and live like a hermit the rest of your life if your wife dies? If any smart alec god gave you a certificate to take another woman on the tenth day after your wife has died, then show it to me![9]

In their different ways, women like Tarabai and Ramabai were already, in the nineteenth century, raising their voices against what Partha Chatterjee has described as the "nationalist resolution of the women's question." This rested on separating the material and cultural spheres and making women the guardians of the home, its moral and spiritual essence: "What was necessary was to cultivate the material techniques of modern western civilization while retaining and strengthening the distinctive spiritual essence of the national culture."[10] In looking to this solution of "eastern morals and western science", there seems to have been no qualitative distinction between reformist Hindus and Hindu nationalists. This was insufficient for women who wanted to be considered complete human beings, since it was the "eastern morals" which oppressed them. (Whether "western morals" also did so is another issue; in fact Ramabai, to take the most obvious example, found herself in many conflicts with her Christian guides regarding attitudes towards women after her conversion.)

Unlike the Arya Samajists, for instance, Ramabai could not see the present state of women simply as "degeneration". Unlike the Brahmo Samajists and men like Gandhi, she could not turn to idealized versions of the Vedas and Upanishads to convince herself that the "essence" of Hindu spiritualism could be saved from its casteist and patriarchal excrescences. Ramabai, like Phule and the later militant dalits, had to reject Hinduism. Similarly, Tarabai could not see rishis and gods as symbols of divinity without accepting her own position as an inferior. Yet how is it that so many of the later and more highly placed women activists came to compromise on these issues? The answer is partly, of course, that they were forced to: compromise was a way to make some small gains.

After the upsurge of Hindu nationalism in the late nineteenth century had forced even the moderate social reformism of the upper castes to retreat, the women's movement slowly took on an organized form. It emerged with some autonomy in the 1920s with the founding of the All-India Women's Congress and similar organizations. These upper caste and elite women's organizations worked within the Hindu framework and spoke of Sita and Savitri as ideals for women, not as symbols of male oppression. They praised the freedom of the Vedic period, and depicted purdah and other evils as resulting from the social conditions of the Muslim invasion, if not from the Muslims themselves. They fought for (and eventually got implemented in some form) a new Hindu code giving substantial, though hardly equal, rights to women in such sensitive areas as property and divorce. But they were embarassed by the fact that a dalit, Ambedkar, was the chairman of its drafting committee; and they had no organization to combat the street demonstrations organized by the fundamentalists. Further, by leaving Muslim women out of the bill, they left a dangerous legacy for the fomentation of communal feelings in later years.[11]

Peasant women seem to have had their own forms of action that reinterpreted tradition more actively but very often also remained within the framework of the Hindu discourse while building an organizational space for women. Kapil Kumar describes the role of women led by Jaggi (a Kurmi) in the Oudh Kisan Sabha, supported by Baba Ramchandra (a Maharashtrian brahman). This led to the founding of a women's front, the Kishanin Sabha, which focused both on giving women land rights, and attacking male polygamy and reforming family relations. Like Phule, the Kisanin Sabha argued for monogomy. Its rules stated that all relationships should be treated as legitimate and that women should be respected even if they did not produce children.[12] In addition, while using local religious traditions (like celebrating a success with a *yagya* to a village goddess), there was also a reinterpretation of tradition. Thus Kaikeyi was praised for sending Rama to the jungle, and Sita was viewed as a woman who acted on her own: "Did not Rama tell Sita not to accompany him to the forest but Sita on her own decided to go?"[13]

There is very little historical evidence, and even less effort to uncover what may exist, of the actual discourse and actions of working class and peasant women throughout this

period while their elite sisters were yielding to the male for-
mulations of Hindu nationalist themes, whether those of
Hindu raj or Ram raj. Sumanta Banerjee offers a clue to what
could be done in his depiction of lower class women's culture in nineteenth-century Calcutta, while talking of the
kheur, a popular form of songs on the Radha-Krishna theme,
which evolved into a kind of drama of repartee. He cites one
example in which Ambalika protests when her mother
Satyavati urges her to have union with Vyasa to beget a
child:

People say
as a girl you used to row a boat in the river.
Seeing your beauty, tempted by your lotus-bud,
the great Parashar stung you, and
there was a hue and cry:
You've done it once,
You don't have anything to fear.
Now you can do as much as you want to,
no one will say anything.
If it has to be done,
Why don't you do it, mother?[14]

Such forms of expression were used by many lower class
women. Similar biting dialogues were apparently also used
in the Satyashodhak *tamashas* of the 1920s in Maharashtra
and seem to have been common to *tamasha* culture in most
parts of India. The logical style of the Ambalika song (if you
think it's so great, do it yourself) provoked an uproar a century later in the intellectual circles of Bombay (at the time of
the founding of the Dalit Panthers in 1972) when a prominent Marathi writer said that "prostitutes do work necessary
to society and so should be given respect", and Raja Dhale
won himself temporary fame, saying, "If Durgabai thinks the
work deserves so much respect, why doesn't she do it herself?"

The powerful critiques of the early feminists, women like Ramabai and Tarabai and their male supporters, focused on crucial issues of patriarchy and sexuality, attacking the double standard of *pativrata*. Many women upheld the value of monogamy and others used legends and mythology to mock all impositions of sexual standards, though no explicit claims to sexual freedom were raised among reformers and radicals. Later leaders of the women's movement during the colonial period, identified with the dominant Hindu reformist cultural trend underlying the Congress organizations and in so doing, accepted the basic framework of brahmanical patriarchy. But it was early feminists like Ramabai and Tarabai who were closer to the general attitude of lower class and peasant women in taking the *puranas* as stories and not scriptures, and seeing them as representing the many facets of male oppression rather than as divinely-ordained ideals of human relationships.

5

Hinduism as Aryan Conquest: The Dalit Radicals of the 1920s

The mobilization of the oppressed and exploited sections of society—the peasants, dalits, women and low castes that Phule had spoken of as *shudras* and *ati-shudras*—occurred on a large scale in the 1920s and 1930s, under varying leaderships and with varying ideologies. They took part in nationalist campaigns, some of them hailing Gandhi as a kind of messianic figure; they organized unions and kisan sabhas; they staged strikes, anti-rent campaigns and revenue/tax boycotts; they fought for forest and village commons. It was an era, following the first World War and the Russian Revolution, when the masses were coming on to the stage of history.

Inevitably, the specificities of caste exploitation could not be ignored in India. Many low-caste activists of the 1920s, organizing as non-brahmans and dalits, were drawn to an anti-caste, anti-brahman, even anti-Hindu ideology of the kind that Phule had formulated. Since few outside Maharashtra had heard of Phule, most likely it was the Tamil non-brahman movement which had the most influence as the strongest initiator of "non-Aryan" themes. Yet so pervasive were these that it is clear the themes struck a deep mass resonance everywhere. The very use of "Aryan" discourse by the elite was evoking a common response which, in its turn, was to force the elite to revise this discourse significantly. The non-brahman movements in Maharashtra and Tamil Nadu, as well as the dalit movements arising in places as distant as the Punjab and Karnataka, all began to argue in terms of the Aryan conquest and brahman exploitation through religion.

Even the names of most dalit movements—Ad-Dharm in Punjab, Adi-Hindu in U.P and Hyderabad, Adi-Dravida, Adi-Andhra and Adi-Karnataka in south India—indicated a common claim to being original inhabitants. This was exemplified early in Maharashtra, where a pre-Ambedkar dalit leader, Kisan Faguji Bansode (1870-1946), warned his caste Hindu friends in 1909 that:

> The Aryans—your ancestors—conquered us and gave us unbearable harassment. At that time we were your conquest, you treated us even worse than slaves and subjected us to any torture you wanted. But now we are no longer your subjects, we have no service relationship with you, we are not your slaves or serfs... We have had enough of the harassment and torture of the Hindus.[1]

Bansode, an educator and journalist, represented a generation of educated Mahar leaders that arose in Nagpur, where Mahars often had some land and formed forty per cent of the workers in an emerging textile industry. He, like many other of the regional Mahar leadership, later turned away from such themes, identifying with Hinduism through devotion to the Mahar saint Chokamela, and Ambedkar in fact had to fight this group to establish his own leadership in Vidarbha.[2] However, by the 1920s, the new dalit or "adi" movements, with an ideological claim to being heirs of a "non-Aryan" or "original Indian" equalitarian tradition, began to take off in many regions of India.

35

In Andhra, where the process was affected by the militant Dravidianism of the Madras presidency, the commercialized coastal areas produced both a mobile dalit agricultural labourer class and a small educated section. A proposed conference of dalits in Vijayawada in 1917, sponsored by reformist Hindus, was to be called the First Provincial Panchama Mahajana Sabha but changed its name, in a mood of revolt, to the Adi-Andhra Mahajana Sabha on the grounds that "the so-called Panchamas were the original sons of the soil and they were the rulers of the country."[3] The dalits were in a militant mood; the major temple in the city closed down for the three days of their conference. For over a decade and a half after that, until they became absorbed as "harijans" into the Congress and Communist movements, coastal Andhra dalits held conferences as Adi- Andhras. By the 1931 census, nearly a third of the Malas and Madigas of the Madras presidency had given their identity as Adi-Andhra.

The Vijayawada conference was presided over by Bhagyareddy Varma (1888-1939), a Hyderabad dalit originally named Madari Bhagaiah, who had been organizing Adi-Hindu conferences since 1912. Hyderabad had a vigorous, though factionalized, petty bourgeois dalit group, which began to pick up the Adi-Hindu identity in the 1920s. By 1930 the state census indicated a rather vigorous cultural debate:

> The Adi-Dravida Educational League argued that, judged by the history, philosophy and civilization of the Adi-Dravidas, the real aborigines of the Deccan, the depressed classes are, as a community, entirely separate and distinct from the followers of Vedic religion, called Hindus. The League's contention was that Hinduism is not the ancestral religion of the aborigines of Hindustan; that the non-Vedic communities of India object to being called Hindu because of their inherited abhorance of the doctrines of the

Manusmruti and like scriptures, who have distinguished themselves from caste Hindus for centuries past, that the Vedic religion which the Aryans brought in the wake of their invasion was actively practiced upon the non-Vedic aborigines, and that the aborigines, coming under the influence of the Hindus, gradually and half-consciously adopted Hindu ideas and prejudices.[4]

In Hyderabad, thus, Tamil dalits identified themselves as Adi-Dravidas. Telugu-speaking dalits called themselves Adi-Hindus but a large section of them gave this a militant, anti-brahman interpretation. Bhagyareddy Varma was a major figure in this group, later identifying with Buddhism and giving tacit support to a younger generation of radicals who became followers of Ambedkar. In faraway U.P. too, where Varma travelled for conferences, a new radical identity arose. Its leading ideologue was an untouchable ascetic from Mainpuri district who had briefly been a member of the Arya Samaj. He left it out of disgust and began to organize the dalits on the basis of an Adi-Hindu identity. Calling himself, rather defiantly, Acchutananda, he argued:

The untouchables, the so-called harijans, are in fact *adi*-Hindu, i.e. the original or autochthonous Nagas or Dasas of the north and the Dravidas of the south of the subcontinent, and they are the undisputed, heavenly owners of Bharat. All others are immigrants to the land, including the Aryans, who conquered the original populations not by valour but by deceit and manipulation ... by usurping others' rights, subjugating the peace-loving and rendering the self-sufficient people indigents and slaves. Those who ardently believed in equality were ranked, and ranked lowest. The Hindus and untouchables have since always remained poles apart.[5]

In Punjab, a dalit named Mangoo Ram, also originally a part of the Arya Samaj, began an Ad-Dharm movement in which the dalits by 1926, had proclaimed themselves a separate *quaum* (community) in a conference in a village of Hoshiarpur district. As the report of the Ad-Dharm Mandal described the Aryan conquest:

> During this time of great achievements, the Aryans heard about the original land's civilization and came there. They learned the art of fighting from the local inhabitants, and then turned against them. There were many wars—six hundred years of fighting—and then the Aryans finally defeated our ancestors, the local inhabitants. Our forefathers ... were pushed back into the jungles and the mountains ... from that time to this time the Hindu Aryans have suppressed the original people.[6]

Again there was a concern for official record of identity. By the 1931 census, nearly 500,000 Ad-Dharmis were reported.

Mangoo Ram, Acchutanand, Bhagyareddy Varma and Kisan Bansode were all of a generation slightly older than Ambedkar. They represented a new movement, they organized on the basis of some mobility of village untouchables—some going into new factories and industries, some overseas to plantations or as soldiers in the Indian army, others claiming small holdings of land deriving from traditional village service-claims or even acquired from factory or other earnings. Spearheading the dalit organizations was a growing, though still small, educated or semi-educated leadership. Various activities were taken up in this period. On the one hand, social reform included efforts to abolish devadasi traditions and sub-caste differences, and giving up drinking or meat-eating. On the other hand, organizing occurred on economic issues concerning factory and mill workers and efforts to acquire land.

While much of this involved linkages with reformist Hindus and acceptance of a basic Hinduist discourse, it was the "adi" ideologies, based on non-Aryan racial theories, that provided the framework for the most militant expressions. It was not that all dalits, let alone all militant non-brahmans, accepted this; there were in every region those who chose instead to identify themselves as Hindus, fighting for temple entry, for instance. A significant set of dalit leaders even went over to the Hindu Mahasabha. But the adi ideologies were pervasive ideas that won a popular base, as census reports show, and expressed the powerful emotional resistance to brahmanism and caste hierarchy that was embodied in dalit organizations everywhere in the colonial period. (They also had links with the themes of the non-brahman movements of the Madras and Bombay presidencies, and most of the militant dalits also had some kind of alliance policy with the non-brahmans.)

However, while these expressions bore similarities to the ideology of Phule, there were crucial differences from Phule's period that were reflected in the 1920s' non-brahman-dalit versions of the non-Aryan themes. First, a whole period of the construction of Hinduism had intervened, with the formulation of an increasingly sophisticated ideology of Hindu nationalism and its spread. The founding of major organizations such as the Hindu Mahasabha and the Rashtriya Swayamsevak Sangh (RSS) occurred in this period. While the RSS remained an aloof, indrawn cadre organization, organizations like the Mahasabha and the Arya Samaj undertook campaigns to win over low castes. The *shuddhi* campaign (designed to "purify" dalits or convert them back from Islam) was carried out primarily in the Punjab, but the ideological appeals that went along with this had a much wider spread. These identified dalits as part of the "Hindu fold", and began to emphasize the low-caste origin of figures such as Valmiki and Vyasa to show that dalits too had a part in the "creation of its great literature". Hindu nationalist upper castes were revising and reinterpreting the racial aspect of their identity to stress a Hindu unity encompassing the caste hierarchy. By the 1930s, it was clear that this reinterpretation had an appeal: not only were large sections of non-brahmans identifying themselves as Hindus and claiming kshatriya status through the medium of caste conferences, but many important dalit leaders were also won over, with some like M.S. Rajah of Tamil Nadu and G.A. Gavai of Nagpur even ready to join the Hindu Mahasabha.

On the other hand, the dalit activists, peasants and workers of the time confronted the formulation of a radical class ideology by a new left intelligentsia. Young Indian socialists and communists led militant struggles that attracted large sections of the exploited and gave them a vision of an equalitarian society, but they avoided the recognition of caste and stressed a mechanical class framework that sought to override traditional identities rather than reinterpret them. It is striking that in the painful confrontation between Gandhi and Ambedkar after the second Round Table Conference, when both Gandhians and Hindu Mahasabhaites tried to mobilize forces against the followers of Ambedkar and promote their solution to the issue, there was no prominent leftist even concerned about caste. Nehru in his autobiography remarks again and again that he saw Gandhi's harijan campaign as diversionary. It led to the diversion of the people's attention from the objective of full independence to the mundane cause of the upliftment of harijans.[7]

There were many aspects of this resistance to dealing with caste. There was an inability to even recognize identities such as the Adi-Andhra; the communists universally adopted the Gandhian term "harijan" without much concern for whether it would appeal to the people concerned. They also saw themselves, without much trouble, as Hindu (perhaps as "Hindu atheists"). At the same time, communist class ideology defined the industrially-employed working class as advanced, while peasants (so crucial to Phule) were seen as backward, either feudal or "petty bourgeois". State exploitation (such as the exploitation of the peasantry by means of taxes and land revenue) was ignored, while only private property owners (moneylenders, zamindars, etc.) were the appropriate objects of class, as opposed to "national" struggle.

As G.P. Deshpande has argued, Phule was making an effort to formulate a kind of universalistic ideology. He did not identify the oppressed and exploited shudras and ati-shudras as a set of castes so much as a peasant community, nor was the community strictly identified in racial terms. Non-Aryan was, after all, a negative category. In the 1920s, in contrast, the communists were putting forward another universalistic ideology. This one did not recognize community/caste as a node of exploitation; it threw all non-class categories into the realm of the superstructure, relegated to secondary consequence since they were only cultural/ideological constructs. *The formation of a class ideology of this type created a caste ideology of a specific type in reaction*, one which set up caste in opposition to class as a cultural/social factor, a non-economic factor.

In this context, with the strong ideological winds of Hindu nationalism (even in the modified form of Gandhism) and class struggle blowing all around them, the alternative "adi" identity theories put forward by dalit radicals became racial ones. This can be seen in the above quotations. The Aryans as a people with one religion (Hinduism) were seen as basically confronting (conquering and enslaving) the non-Aryans as a people with a different religion. Sometimes the conquering Aryan caste/community was seen in larger terms (as "all-caste Hinduism"), sometimes in smaller terms (only as the "upper castes"), but, more often, it was

41

increasingly seen as a racially and religiously solidified group, "the Hindus" Phule had refused to legitimize Hinduism even as the religion of the supposed upper castes, seeing it only as a tool of exploitation. The later radicals also condemned Hinduism but began to see it more and more as a reality.

The communists saw the national movement as basically the only valid non-class struggle of the period, progressive because imperialism had to be fought in order to achieve a democratic revolution that would advance the development of the productive forces (i.e. industrialization). This resulted in the dalit and non-brahman movements being stigmatized as pro-British, the communists refusing to recognize the legitimacy of taking the fight against the Indian elite (or "Indian feudalism") as central.

Thus two opposing ideologies prevailed among the toiling masses, one arguing from the standpoint of being original inhabitants or non-Aryans, and the other basing itself on the theory of class struggle. With the failure, in particular, of the more all-encompassing Marxist theory to incorporate the problems of caste in India, the broad movement of the oppressed was split into a class movement and a caste movement. There was no synthesis, no development of an integrated ideology and, as a result, those lower castes/classes who did get drawn into the national struggle or the left-led working class movement, gave up the sharpness of their anti-caste fight. Beneath the folds of the Congress and its hegemonic claim over almost all other political movements, a large number of forces and identities simmered but remained unconnected and ineffective.

The most significant attempt to transcend this fragmentation in the 1930s and 1940s was made by Dr. B.R. Ambedkar, one of the great democratic leaders of the twentieth century.

6

Hinduism as Counter-Revolution: B.R. Ambedkar

> It must be recognized that there never has been a common Indian culture, that historically there have been three Indias, Brahmanic India, Buddhist India and Hindu India, each with its own culture.... It must be recognized that the history of India before the Muslim invasions is the history of a mortal conflict between Brahmanism and Buddhism.[1]

Dr. Bhimrao Ramji Ambedkar (1891-1956; known as "Babasaheb" in the movement) came into politics claiming the heritage of the non-brahman movement. Between 1917-20 he returned to India after getting his degree in law in the U.S. He gave up service in Baroda state after insults were heaped upon him as an untouchable. Settling in Bombay as a professor at Sydenham College, he associated with Shahu Maharaj of Kolhapur (notorious to nationalists as anti-brahman and pro-British) in his initial political organizing. The autonomy of the dalit movement was his concern, but it was to be an autonomy in alliance with non-brahmans. At the first Depressed Classes conference in Nagpur in 1920, which he attended in the company of Shahu Maharaj, he attacked not only nationalist spokesmen, but also Vitthal Ramji

Shinde,the most prominent non-dalit social reformer claiming to lead the "uplift of untouchables"

Ambedkar's emergence into politics was cautious. Very gradually he gathered a team around him, of educated and semi-educated Mahar boys, as well as a few upper-caste sympathizers, forming the Bahishkrut Hitakarni Sabha, which began to hold conferences around the province. In 1926, an explosive movement resulted when a conference at Mahad in the Konkan ended with a struggle to drink water from the town tank. The Mahad satyagraha, the first "untouchable liberation movement," did not succeed in getting water but did end with the public burning of the Manusmruti. The campaign was partly spontaneous and partly planned; Mahad had been chosen as a place where Ambedkar had significant caste Hindu support, where a tenant movement uniting Mahar and Kunbi peasants was beginning (which developed into the biggest anti-landlord movement in Maharashtra in the 1930s), and where the municipality had already passed a resolution to open public places to untouchables.

By the time of the Simon Commission Ambedkar had clearly emerged as the most articulate dalit leader in the country with a significant mass base, and it was natural that he should be invited to the Round Table Conference. This led to the clash with Gandhi over the issue of an award of separate electorates to untouchables. For Gandhi, the integrity of Hindu society with the untouchables as its indissoluble part was a central and emotional question. The confrontation over Gandhi's fast and the Poona Pact (1932) disillusioned Ambedkar once and for all about Hindu reformism; it inaugurated his radical period which led to an announcement in 1935 that he was "born a Hindu but would not die a Hindu" and the founding in 1936, of the Independent Labour Party (ILP), a worker-peasant party with a red flag. The "conversion announcement" set off ferment throughout the country, while the ILP went on to become the biggest opposition party in the Bombay legislative council.

The 1930s was a decade of ferment, with growing nationalist agitations and workers' and peasants' struggles. The ILP grew and became the only party in India which led struggles against capitalists and landlords along with agitations against caste oppression, calling for a radical opposition to the "brahman-bourgeois Congress" and seeking to pull in non-brahmans as well as dalits. While Ambedkar himself did not support a non-Aryan theory of dalit-shudra identity, poems and songs published in his weekly *Janata* show how pervasive these ideas were, and how they linked anti-caste radicalism with calls for class struggle:

Bhils, Gonds, Dravids, their Bharat was beautiful,
They were the people, the culture was theirs, the rule
*   was theirs;*
The Aryas infiltrated all this, they brought their
*   power to Bharat*
and Dravidans were suppressed...
Brahmans, Kshatriyas, Vaishyas, all became owners
Drinking the blood of slaves, making the Shudras into
*   machines.*
The Brahmans, Kshatriyas and Banias got all the
*   ownership rights.*
All these three call themselves brothers, they come
*   together in times of crisis*
And work to split the Shudras who have become workers.
"Congress," "Hindu Mahasabha," "Muslim League" are
*   all agents of the rich,*
The "Independent Labour Party" is our true house...
*Take up the weapon of **Janata***
Throw off the bloody magic of the owners' atrocities,
Rise workers! Rise peasants! Hindustan is ours,

Humanity will be built on labour,
This is our birth right![2]

The ILP led some major combined struggles in this period. The most notable of these was the anti-landlord agitation in the Konkan region of Maharashtra which brought together Kunbi and Mahar tenants against mainly brahman (but also some upper-caste Maratha) landlords, climaxing in a march of some 25,000 peasants to Bombay in 1938. This was followed by a massive one-day united textile workers' strike against the "black bill" of the Congress government which outlawed strikes. Communists were involved in both of these, and at the massive peasant rally Ambedkar proclaimed, though very ambiguously, an admiration for Marxism:

> I have definitely read studiously more books on the Communist philosophy than all the Communist leaders here. However beautiful the Communist philosophy is in these books ... the test of it has to be given in practice. And if work is done from that perspective, I feel that the labour and length of time needed to win success in Russia will not be so much needed in India ... in regard to the toilers class struggle, I feel the Communist philosophy to be closer to us.[3]

The 1930s was thus the period in which Ambedkar expressed most strongly his major themes of unity and militancy: unity of workers and peasants, of dalits and non-brahmans (shudras), and unity with opposition parties against the Congress. It is striking that all through this period (as later) it was the dominant caste peasants who were the main perpetrators of atrocities against dalits in villages, and the latter under Ambedkar fought this vigorously. Nevertheless at a broader level he called for and tried to build a unity of dalits with the Kunbi-Marathas, associated with the non-brahman party and praised Shahu Maharaj as well as Phule. Ambedkar's position here was that at the caste level, brahmanism was the main enemy, just as capitalism and landlordism were the main enemies in class terms. He consistently argued for the left and non-brahman/dalit forces to come together to form a political alternative that would fight both the Indian ruling classes and imperialism. Thus, for example, following the 1938 peasant and worker struggles, he met with Periyar and Swami Sahajanand, the peasant leader of Bihar, in an attempt to form a broad front. Similarly, he tried to dissuade the non-brahman leaders of Maharashtra from merging their movement with the Congress, arguing that it would only make them the "hamals" or coolies of a brahman leadership.

Yet the 1930s failed to consolidate a radical alternative to the Congress. Apart from the ability of the Congress under Gandhi to win mass support, the main barrier was the argument of the left that the main contradiction was with imperialism and that the Congress represented an "anti-imperialist united front." The movements dissolved, the Communists supported the British Government during the 'anti-fascist' war, and Ambedkar retreated from his radicalism to turn the ILP, which had been limited only to Maharashtra, into a much narrower but more all-India Scheduled Caste Federation (founded 1942). His goal now was to get whatever concessions he could from the British out of an independence he now saw as inevitable. He rapidly accepted a position as Labour Minister in the British government, then as Law Minister in the independent regime of Nehru. Ambedkar still saw the Congress as a 'brahman-bourgeois' party, but since there was little he could do about it he turned to reformist interest-group politcs.

Ambedkar had always seen the necessity of both economic and social measures for the liberation of the dalits. But the acceptance of a mechanical Marxist framework led him to see these as separate entities and not interwoven in the way that Phule had. On the economic front, he mostly began to follow a Nehruvian-left line. While he had written two major books in the early 1920s on fiscal and monetary policy which by and large reflected a neoclassical perspective though with a severe critique of British rule; in the 1930s and 1940s he switched to a socialistic framework that took for granted the necessity of state-guided industrial development but did not confront the problem of high-caste domination over the state machinery. This was expressed in his book *States and Minorities*, written as a submission to the constitutional convention on behalf of the Scheduled Caste Federation. Economics, though, was not by this time his major concern. He was putting most of his intellectual energy into the question of the historical roots of the caste system and India's cultural identity.

Ambedkar began with a rejection not only of Marxist "class theory" but also of the kind of "caste thoery" represented by the non-Aryan identity claims of other dalit radicals of his time. This was seen in two books published during his lifetime, *Who were the Shudras?* and *The Untouchables*, and but it was his unpublished manuscripts, *Revolution and Counter-Revolution in Ancient India* and *The Untouchables: Children of India's Ghetto* which show the breadth of his attempt to articulate a historical theory. *Revolution and Counter-Revolution* represents his major theoretical analysis, and begins with a firm rejection of the Aryan theory of caste: "The Aryans were not a race. The Aryans were a collection of people. The cement that held these together was their interest in the maintenance of a type of culture called Aryan culture."[4] As he had earlier made clear:

> As a matter of fact the caste system came into being long after the different races of India had commingled

in blood and culture. To hold that distinctions of caste are really distinctions of race and to treat different castes as though they were so many different races is a gross perversion of the facts. What affinity is there between the Brahman of the Punjab and the Brahman of Madras? What affinity is there between the Untouchable of Bengal and the Untouchable of Madras?... The Brahman of the Punjab is racially the same stock as the Chamar of the Punjab and the Brahman of Madras is the same race as the Pariah of Madras. Caste system does not demarcate racial division.[5]

It was not that Ambedkar denied "racial" elements completely; for example, he referred to the early Magadha-Mauryan empires as being the work of "Nagas". He simply argued they should not be given causal priority in explaining caste. In his view, all the varnas included some kind of racial mixture; for instance the original "shudras" were a tribe of kshatriya Aryans who had been degraded due to conflicts with brahmans, only later being assimilated with the conquered darker-skinned non-Aryans. Similarly he rejected an analysis in terms of economic factors. In his famous phrase, somewhat similiar to the way he discussed race, "caste is not a division of labour; it is a division of labourers."

Caste was thus neither racial nor economic. What then were the main explanatory factors, the motive of historical change that produced the caste system, this "social division of the people"? With class and race rejected, and violence ignored, the emphasis is on ideological and religious factors. In Ambedkar's analysis these are interwoven as civilizational forces that produced the conflicts and changes in Indian society. Without a knowledge of the Indus valley civilization, he differentiated three major phases, as noted above, with the central element in them being the conflict between Hinduism as representing inequalitarian and oppressive elements, and

49

Buddhism as the advanced, egalitarian and rational mode: (1) brahmanism (the Vedic period, basically tribal in nature and characterized by *varna* among the Vedic Aryans, though this was not based on birth); (2) the "revolutionary" period of Buddhism, marked by the rise of the Magadha and Mauryan states and bringing about a great advance in the status of women and shudras whose position had become degraded in the last stages of the Vedic period; and (3) the "counter-revolutionary" period of Hinduism marked by the Manusmruti, the transformation of *varna* into caste, and the complete downgrading of shudras and women.[6]

> The triumphant Brahmanism began an onslaught on both the Shudras and the women in pursuit of the old idea, namely servility, and Brahmanism did succeed in making the Shudras and the women the servile classes: Shudras the serfs to the three higher classes and the women the serfs to their husbands. Of the black deeds committed by Brahmanism after its triumph over Buddhism this one is the blackest. There is no parallel in history for so foul deeds of degradation committed by a class of usurpers in the name of class domination.[7]

It has to be noted here that in using the term 'shudra' Ambedkar was clearly not referring to the untouchables, whom he saw as "broken men" settled outside the villages; he was referring to the non-brahman masses whom he saw, along with untouchables and tribals, as victims of the caste system. By the 1940s, however, his hope that there would be a unified struggle was at a low ebb, and he was in his political writings treating "Hindus" as a "majority" that included non-brahmans and was posed against such minorities as Muslims and dalits.

Nevertheless, Ambedkar's longer-term strategy was to break up that majority, to dissolve "Hinduism" itself, and to do so by building a unity of dalits and middle castes (non-brahmans) which would be both a caste and a class unity of peasants and workers, against the brahman-bourgeois Congress. The last years of his life saw a return to this kind of united front, expressed in the change of his Scheduled Caste Federation into the (hopefully non-caste) Republican Party. It participated in the Samyukta Maharashtra Samiti, organized to fight for a Marathi-speaking state and which was actually the first full left-democratic front of opposition parties. Ambedkar, in fact, had argued that the united front should continue even after the winning of a Marathi-speaking state, and fight for the interests of the rural poor; and a massive land satyagraha led by his lieutenant Dadasaheb Gaikwad and communist peasant leaders followed in both 1956 and 1965.

Yet, the end of Ambedkar's life is remembered by the masses of his dalit followers neither for the class unity of peasants and workers nor for the renewed effort at forming the Republican Party as a broad-based organization but for his conversion to Buddhism along with nearly a million dalits in Nagpur. For Ambedkar, and for the militant dalits who followed him, Hinduism remained in the final analysis a religion of caste that had to be renounced and destroyed if the masses of India were to win liberation. He had written in 1936, in confrontation with Gandhi and Punjab anti-caste radicals, that it was necessary to deal with religion. Indian socialists, he noted:

> will be compelled to take account of caste after the revolution if (they) do not take account of it before revolution. This is only another way of saying that, turn in any direction you like, caste is the monster that crosses your path. You cannot have political reform, you cannot have economic reform, unless you kill this monster.[8]

But this, he went on to argue, required that "you must destroy the Religion of the Shrutis and the Shastras. Nothing else will succeed."[9] "You will succeed in saving Hinduism if you kill Brahmanism," he argued, softening his blow with suggested reforms for Hinduism. It is perhaps this kind of language that has provided a thin wedge for the BJP to try to co-opt even Ambedkar as a "Hindu reformer." But such Hindu reformism would have required the rejection of all the sacred books of the Hindus, of Rama and Krishna as ideals, and in the end Ambedkar was unwilling to believe this was possible. His unpublished writings are harsh in their overall critique:

> Is there then no principle in Hinduism [to] which all Hindus, no matter what their other differences are, feel bound to render willing obedience? It seems to me there is, and that principle is the principle of caste.[10]

The way to liberation, then, involved economic and ideological struggle, and Ambedkar never gave up the former. But his stress was on ideological/cultural struggle, and though he could not succeed in fully integrating it with an economic alternative, he gave it a sharpness that would remain: the challenge before socialists—to deal with the "monster that would always cross their path," the issue of caste and its religious justifications.

7

Hinduism as Delhi Rule: Periyar and the National Question

As the colonial period drew to an end the surface waves of Indian politics were dominated by the issue of Muslim separatism and Hindu identity. Hinduism came to be a taken-for-granted identity, whether it was the moderate and liberal version most Congressmen subscribed to, or the increasingly virulent form of Hindu nationalism. The latter, growing throughout the 1920s and 1930s, began increasingly to emphasize not only blood and territory (race, religion and nation) but also language, projecting Sanskrit/Hindi as the quintessentially "Indian" languages. This had a significant north Indian bias. *Hindi-Hindu-Hindustan*, the emotive slogan of north Indian fundamentalism, had a powerful negative side: the equation of language, religion and nation encouraged not only those with a different religious identity but also those with a separate linguistic identity to see themselves as a different "nation". Thus the other side of the powerful centralizing tendency of Hindu fundamentalism was that many anti-caste movements turned to a regional and anti-northern, as well as anti-brahman identification.

Caste is not ethnicity, and Ambedkar above all had insisted on this distinction and taken a resolutely all-Indian, even centralist attitude. But caste, community and ethnicity have common features, also seen in the vernacular meanings of *jati* and *quaum*, which are often overlapping. From the time of Phule a broad stream in the anti-caste movement had stressed these, seeing the brahmanic elites as Aryan and themselves as non-Aryan, of a different ethnic community and even a different race. Given the diversity of India, reflected especially in the diversity of the non-brahman and dalit communities, it is not surprising that these mass ethnic identities got expressed in different forms in different regions. The opposition to "brahman" and "Hindu" then got reflected in varying non-Hindi and sometimes anti-north Indian nationality identifications.

By the 1930s, for example, Sikh and Muslim religious identities were also taking on regional/nationalist aspects and in the process opposed Congress domination as Hindu domination and "brahman-bania rule". The caste discourse of the opposition helped to link them to the non-brahman and dalit movements and perhaps provided a ground for the alliances that were taking place. In the 1930s for instance, Mangoo Ram of the Punjab allied with the Unionist Party and the Namashudras with the Krishak Praja Party in Bengal. At the same time the strong Hindu-Muslim antagonisms which were developing especially in north India were, in many other regions getting diversified into demands for regional separation and autonomy. By the late 1940s the movement for Pakistan was feeding that for Dravidistan and similar trends could be seen elsewhere. Anti-Hinduism was taking on a rather complex, anti-northern, anti-centralist character.

Developments in Tamil Nadu provide an insight into the process. Here was a strongly independent Dravidian linguistic identity and a long history of being the southern centre of the subcontinent, not only unconquered by northerners but a centre of empires of its own, stretching sometimes overseas and oriented in many ways more towards south-east Asia in contrast to the northern west Asian linkages. Here, since the late nineteenth century, anti-brahmanism had the built-in claim of being the non-Aryan original inhabitants of the land. This led to an idealization of ancient Tamil society; Saivaism, or the Saiva Siddhanta philosophy was posed as an indigenous, even non-Hindu religion. This was to form the basis for claiming an identity as Dravidians and, by the 1940s and 1950s for Tamil nationalism.

The early non-brahman movement in Tamil Nadu was more elite-based than in Maharashtra with the relatively high-caste Vellalas and other non-brahman landlords and professionals from the Telugu and Malayalam speaking regions able to confront the brahmans on their own footing, increasingly without having to build much of a mass movement.[1] But, by the 1920s a new, militant, mass-oriented movement arose. Its leader was E.V. Ramaswami, 'Periyar' (1879-1973), from a merchant family of Erode. He had joined the Congress in 1919, then gradually became disillusioned with what he saw as its brahmanic leadership. In the early 1920s he took part in the Vaikom temple satyagraha, reportedly clashing with Gandhi while taking a militant position. He later argued that Gandhi had pushed him out of the satyagraha when he engineered a compromise. Nonetheless, Periyar returned to Tamil Nadu as the "hero of Vaikom." He subsequently clashed with Congress leaders over a proposed resolution for reservations in legislatures for non-brahmans and untouchables. In 1925 Periyar left the Congress. In 1927 during a tour of south India Gandhi defended *varnashrama dharma* and Periyar contested this hotly, in personal meetings and in articles in his journal *Kudi Arasu*. He now claimed that three conditions were necessary for the country to gain its freedom: destruction of the Congress, of the so-called Hindu religion, and of brahman domination.[2]

Periyar formed the Self-Respect League in 1926 and its
first conference was held in 1929 making it a Tamil Nadu-
wide movement. Its focus was similar to that of Phule's
Satyashodhak Samaj, opposing brahman priesthood, calling
for the abolition of caste, and supporting the liberation of
women. He attacked all religions more than Phule did, taking an atheistic stance that contrasted with the modified
Saivaism of the non-brahman elite:

> There is no god,
> there is no god,
> there is no god at all.
> He who invented god is a fool.
> He who propagates god is a scoundrel.
> He who worships god is a barbarian.

The dialectic between Phule's theism and Periyar's atheism was in a sense duplicated in the small state of Kerala
where Narayanaswami Guru's "one religion, one caste, one
god" was opposed by his atheistic disciple Ayyapan with the
slogan "no religion, no caste and no god for mankind". The
radical nationalism of the Self-Respect Movement inspired
many at the time, among them the poet Bharati Dasan who
published his first collection in 1938 which invoked "original" Tamil values not as in the sense of seeking a revival-
istic return to a golden age but as an inspiration for an
autonomous modernity:

> . Is it greatness to refuse the right of women
>   Or is it great to be happy with the progress of
>   women?
> Is it right that women marry out of love,
>   Or is it right that we kill them after performing a
>   child marriage?
> Is it right to believe in the Vedas, in God, in all this
>   decay?

56

Or is it right to establish socialism on earth?
Will we live continuing the divisions which surround us?
Or will we live rising up through self-respect?[3]

Bharati Dasan's socialism reflected a new radicalism and a temporary coming together of anti-caste and class themes in the early 1930s. On the one hand, Periyar's equalitarianism, anti-caste radicalism and atheism, all expressed in powerful Tamil speeches, were attracting a group of militant lower-caste youth, giving a new invigoration to the old non-brahman movement and radicalizing it. On the other hand, a sparking role was played by Singaravelu, a union leader from a fish workers' caste who is considered the "first Communist of south India," and indeed was the first Indian to independently form a labour party, considered a forerunner of the Communist Party.[4]

In 1932, Periyar toured the Soviet Union and was impressed by the concrete accomplishments of atheistic socialism while Singaravelu wrote a series of articles in *Kudi Arasu* expounding socialism and a materialistic interpretation of history. On Periyar's return, he and Singaravelu placed a new programme before Self-Respect activists in December 1932 and it was suggested that a political party be formed, using the name Samadharma party as the closest Tamil equivalent to "socialism". Socialism now began to be propagated from Self-Respect platforms, while anti-landlord and anti-moneylender conferences were held by non-brahman activists.

But this coming together of the left and anti-caste movements seemed doomed from the beginning. On the one hand conservatives in the non-brahman movement opposed it, and when in 1933 Periyar was arrested and jailed, it was clear that British pressure was on. On the other hand, Communist leaders, centred in Bombay, regarded any dilution of a class line with suspicion. Singaravelu's type of indigenous socialism, identified with dangerous non-class forces such as the anti-caste movement and regional-national identities, had to be kept under a tight rein. Singaravelu (then in his seventies) began to argue by 1934 that the term Samadharma should be dropped and the movement openly identify itself as socialist. The real split, though, was on a straightforward political issue: whether, in the 1934 elections, with no socialist party around, the Self-Respect movement should support the Justice Party or the Congress. Periyar saw his political future in a revival and radicalization of the Justice Party. The left could see it only in the Congress, which by 1935 they were identifying explicitly as the "anti-imperialist united front". In 1936, the Communist leadership ordered Singaravelu and others to dissolve their organization and instead join the Congress Socialist Party, a part of the solidly all-Indian National Congress within which the Communists were working. Dange's speech at the conference which dissolved the movement stressed the dangers of linguistic nationalism: "He reminded the conference that not only Tamil Nadu but the whole of India is under British imperialist domination, and that unless the bondage of India under British imperialism is destroyed on an all-India scale it is impossible even to dream of socialism."[5]

The result of young radical communist cadres leaving the movement was to deprive it of a class thrust. As Periyar and his co-workers clashed with the "brahmanic" left, they increasingly identified with a linguistic nationalism. In the south it was easy to give a specific ethnic and national identity to non-Aryan: the people obviously had a language with a non-European origin and the original inhabitants were Dravidian or Tamil. Phule had attacked the story of Vishnu's avatars as representing an external, Aryan conquest of the subcontinent; Periyar described it as a conquest of the south by the north. Phule had taken Bali Raja, the mythological "peasant king," as a hero; the Tamils took Ravana as the

symbol of the south. In this they were only following popular Ramayana traditions. Ravana is seen as hero in many
non-Valmiki versions of the epic in south and west India,
south east Asia and even Kashmir. The versions emphasize
love and war, the heroism and tragic fate of Ravana, in contrast to the feudal, patriarchal and hierarchical values emphasized by the Chinese and north Indian versions centred
around Rama.

By the 1940s, Tamil/Dravidian nationalistic themes were
coming to dominate opposition politics. In 1936 a Congress
government (headed by Rajagopalacharya) came to power in
Madras Province as in most parts of India. As Congress began what Sumit Sarkar has described as "a steady shift to
the Right, occasionally veiled by 'Left' rhetoric,"[6] organizations of peasants and workers went on the offensive in many
parts of the country. In Madras as well, strikes and campaigns took place, but the split between Periyar and the communists meant that there was no coordination of the
class-caste struggle, not even a search for a common ground.
Periyar himself was hardly an ideologue, and took only passing interest in economic issues. Without socialist cadres to
push him on, he began to organize constant campaigns
against the imposition of Hindi, stressing the theme of
Dravidian/Tamil nationality. With the rise of the demand
for Pakistan the movement gained strength, and in 1939 the
Dravida Nadu Conference for the Advocacy of a Separate
and Independent Dravidastan, demanded a separate country
along the lines of Pakistan.[7]

Regional nationalism was beginning to grow in various
parts of India. The demand for Pakistan itself was from the
beginning conceived not simply in religious terms but in
religious-territorial terms identified with the northwest: the
earliest version spoke of "Pakistan, Hindustan and Bengal,"
and the one proposed in 1938-39 included Hyderabad to
make up four independent states. By the 1940s Jinnah was

willing to include Dravidastan as one of the four regions.[8]
The 1938-39 proposal reflected a vigorous campaign in
Hyderabad sponsored by the Nizam to promote a composite
Hindu-Muslim "Deccani" culture as a basis for identity. This
could win over a few prominent dalit leaders, though it was
ultimately compromised by its association with a feudal regime and could withstand neither Hindu nor Muslim fundamentalism.

Similarly, Sikh/Punjabi identity was expressing itself
both in regional and religious terms, by sharing with the
non-brahmans an antagonism towards brahmans and banias.
In Kashmir, Muslim Kashmiris were beginning to conceptu-
alize their identity not simply in religious but in re-
gional/ethnic terms, as "Kashmiriat" Even in the far
north-east, the educated Assamese stressed an anti-Bengali
identity while identifying with Hinduism (Vaishnavism), the
tribals of the plains were questioning both Assamese high-
caste identification and asserting a specific north-eastern
identity. This identity carried. the sense of being Mongoloid
in contrast with the Aryan identities of high-caste Assamese
Hindus as well as Muslims. A first convention of the All-
Assam Tribes and Races Federation in 1945 unanimously
resolved that:

> In view of the fact that historically, Assam proper,
> with its hills, was never a part or province of India
> and that its people, particularly the Tribes and Races
> inhabiting it are ethnically and culturally different
> from the people of the rest of India, this convention
> is emphatically opposed to Assam proper with its
> hills being included into any proposed division of
> India, Pakistan or Hindustan, and demands that it
> should be constituted into a separate Free State into
> which the Hill Districts bordering Assam be incorp-
> orated.[9]

'Subnational' identities were thus becoming a major undercurrent of politics in the 1940s. They did not, it should be noted, always imply a separatist nationalism; they could also lead to demands for autonomy coupled with a loose federal centre. Thus, for instance, the leader of the Unionist Party in the Punjab, Sikandar Hayat Khan, rejected Pakistan as the equivalent of a "Muslim raj" and suggested instead a three-tier structure with autonomous provinces grouped into seven regions, these joined in a loose confederation in which the centre had charge only over defence, external affairs, currency and customs.[10] This type of autonomy was to be the demand with which Sheikh Abdullah's National Conference agreed to Kashmir joining the Indian Union; and it was to be revived after independence in both Punjab and Kashmir—intermittently with movements for independent states.

Meanwhile Periyar had decided to focus on the question of India's future and succeeded in building a political organization that would become the major party in Tamil Nadu. In 1944 he revived the Justice Party, changed its name to Dravida Kazhagham (DK) and declared its goal to be a "sovereign, independent Dravidian Republic". The flag adopted was black with a red circle. Independence was declared a "day of mourning" for representing the enslavement of the southerners"[11] Several strands were brought together by the DK with their focal point being Tamil nationalism:

> We want our country;
> Change the name to Tamil Nadu;
> All-India Union Government means a government
>   protecting Hindu religion;
> We must leave the Hindu Delhi.[12]

Tamil nationalism, linked with the anti-caste movement, thus became a powerful force in the south. However it could win none of its major demands. The post-independence Congress government succeeded in diluting the radicalism of the

Dravidian forces. The DK gave birth to the Dravida Munnetra Kazhagham (DMK) which gave up the separatist demand, and then to the All-India Dravida Munnetra Kazhagham (AIADMK) which capitalized on the charisma of its superstar leader and asserted an all-India identity, allied with Congress and eventually propped up its dead hero's film star companion as a temperamental dictatorial leader. The major problem of the Dravidian movement remained the difficulty of winning dalit support, something Phule had put at the centre of his strategy. In Tamil Nadu, it was not the radical Ambedkar but the Hindu Mahasabhaite M.C. Rajah who was the most well-known dalit leader, and his alienation from the Dravidian movement was the other side of the distancing of the movement itself from dalits. The south thus witnessed a powerful non-brahman movement and a strong opposition to "Hinduism" but more than in any other region was plagued by splits between communists and Dravidians, and dalits and non-brahmans.

The currents of regional or subnational (linguistic national) identity were thus significant during the colonial period. They overlapped in complicated ways with claims to a non-Hindu religious identity, but they nearly always shared a framework of opposition to a brahman-bania, Delhi-based centralized rule. The logical outcome of these movements was not necessarily towards the establishment of an independent nation-state; demands for independence were often raised, but the thrust was just as much on a decentralized, federal structure with much more autonomous regions than in the Indian union which came into existence. The triumph of the Congress finally represented both a triumph of a "Hindu" identity and of a centralized, Delhi-based state in the Indian subcontinent.

8

Brahman Socialism and the Hindu Rate of Growth

During the colonial period the overwhelmingly brahman Indian elite fashioned an upgraded "Hinduism" which rein-terpreted Indian identity and Indian history in a way that could draw low castes, women, adivasis and others into a "national community" whose core was conceived to be the Vedic, Aryan, brahmanic tradition. Whether it was Tilak and the Ganapati festival, Vivekananda and Ramakrishna, or Dayananda and the Arya Samaj, largely high-caste symbols were used to define the heart of this tradition. Even after Hindutva theorists began to argue that the Aryans actually originated in the subcontinent, the notion of Aryans as a core group was kept. And, while the militant "Hindu national-ists" of the RSS and Hindu Mahasabha gave this a more virulent anti-Muslim character by making Hinduism the centre of the Indian state, there were disturbing similarities between their imaging of Indian history and that of pro-claimed secularists such as Nehru or even Dange.

While continuing to use such emotive Hindu terminology as Ram Raj and identifying himself fully with this tradition, Gandhi nevertheless sought to give it a major reinterpreta-tion by proclaiming non-violence and truth as its core. He also offered the basis for a different path of development with his notion of *gram swaraj* and a decentralized, village-centred economy. But this was so inextricably linked with Ram Raj and Hindu-Vedantist anti-technological and anti-sexual ideas of limiting wants, as to discredit it among those—like Ambedkar—concerned with rationality and a need to lift Indians out of their current, colonially-induced poverty.

In the end Gandhi fell a victim to the Hindu nationalists themselves who were furious at what they saw as his responsibility for Partition. Yet, ironically, contemporary "revisionist" historical scholarship is stressing the role of the Congress leadership in choosing Partition, since a united India would inevitably have been a decentralized and federated one giving too many concessions to the Muslim-majority areas and only a truncated India could offer the centralized state structure they demanded.[1]

Forces countering the Hindu majority interpretation of Indian society and history existed throughout the colonial period, pre-dating the overriding preoccupation with the "Muslim problem". This is clearly shown in the work of Jotiba Phule. But these forces were fragmented and remained subordinated. The Communists themselves who claimed to be the main "class" opposition to the "bourgeois" Congress could not offer a serious challenge at the level of mass mobilization, in spite of their considerable working class base and such sporadic tempests as the Telengana revolt. Worse, they never even tried to counter its Hinduist interpretation of history, with the most well known Communist excursion into historical interpretation, Dange's *India: From Primitive Communism to Slavery*, also beginning with the Aryans. The non-brahman/Satyashodhak movement in Maharashtra was absorbed in the 1930s; that in Tamil Nadu evolved into a more long-lasting Dravidian movement but one which was even more split from left and dalit trends. The radical voices of early feminists were buried under the weight of a more compromising and upper class pre-independence women's movement. The peripheries, such as the north-east, remained remote, without influence on "all India" developments. In this context, the dalit movement from the 1920s sought to carry on a cultural and economic challenge to the dominant elite, but the efforts of leaders like Ambedkar and numerous others throughout the country had no hopes of achieving hegemony on their own, without the basic shudra–atishudra unity which Phule had projected and which Ambedkar also wished to build.

It was the Congress which triumphed. The usual categorization of the Congress by the left, as representing some form of "bourgeois" (national, monopoly, comprador) or "bourgeois-landlord" force, simply misses much reality. Ambedkar's "bourgeois-brahman" or more aptly bourgeois (bania)-bureaucratic (brahman) would be more accurate. With the assassination of Gandhi marking the end of an era of struggle, the suave and sophisticated Nehru was the natural leader of the party. With the Second Five-Year Plan a "socialist pattern of development"—a focus on heavy industrialization and the state sector—was chosen. This was influenced by the powerful successes claimed by the Soviet Union, by the overwhelming swing of all newly independent countries towards state-controlled development, and by a consensus even among "development economists" on such issues. But the "Nehru model" had its specific Hindu character from the beginning. As Nehru himself described the choice of socialism over capitalism:

> The old culture managed to live through many a fierce storm and tempest, but, though it kept its outer form, it lost its real content. Today it is fighting silently and desperately against a new and all-powerful opponent—the *bania* civilization of the capitalist West. It will succumb to this newcomer, for the West brings

science and science brings food for the hungry millions. But the West also brings an antidote to the evils of this cut-throat civilization—the principles of socialism for cooperation, and service to the community for the common good. This is not so unlike the old Brahman ideal of service, but it means the brahmanization (not in the religious sense, of course) of all classes and groups and the abolition of class distinctions. It may be that when India puts on her new garment, as she must, for the old is torn and tattered, she will have it cut in this fashion, so as to make it conform both to present conditions and her old thought.[2]

The left critique of Congress socialism has been that it was capitalist reformism because it did not admit of working class leadership. This is insufficient. It was worse than that. It was brahmanism, of course idealized by Nehru in terms of "service" and "cooperation", but with a clear implication that these meant management; socialism was identified with planning and the public sector, with statism. That it could mean something very different, the rule of the shudras (the working classes), never seems to have occurred to Nehru. The only thing he had against the Gandhian notion of "trusteeship", apparently, was that it could be that of private capitalists, the hated banias. Brahmanic trusteeship in the hands of a public sector was another matter.

Gandhi had opposed a heavy industrially-powered development, arguing that "by using Manchester cloth we only waste our money; but by reproducing Manchester in India we save our money at the price of our blood because our very moral being will be sapped."[3] "Reproducing Manchester", only under state ownership, was precisely what India's new ruling elite set out to do. Neither Gandhi nor any of the well-known Gandhian economists could offer a rational basis for a decentralized development; Gandhism remained at the moral level, and efforts to promote khadi and village industries remained a matter of government patronage which had little to do with real self reliance. Industrialization was a goal no third world country rejected; and the over-whelming consensus of development theory at the time of Indian independence made the Nehru-Mahalanobis type of planning and the focus on the public sector practically inevit-able. But the costs of the path not taken were borne by a major section of the toiling people whose poverty remained as oppressive as ever.

The brahmanic socialism of the Nehruvian model of de-velopment created a powerful superstructure—a heavy in-dustrial base, a scientific and technological establishment, an extensive university system, a glittering cultural scene. The growth rate it involved, aptly nicknamed the "Hindu rate of growth" by economist Raj Krishna was, at 3.5 per cent, quite respectable by previous history of economic growth but was barely 1.5 per cent per capita annually in the first three dec-ades after independence: it rose slightly in the 1980s so that the per capita growth rate was 1.9 per cent from 1965-1990. But this was significantly lower than the 2.9 per cent for all other low income countries and 5.8 per cent for China in the same period. As the South Commission put it,

> Growth was not high enough to trickle down ... in India, growth in the first three post-war decades was much slower than the average for the developing countries. The rise in India's per capita income, of the order of about 1.5 per cent per year, was too small to secure a significant improvement in the living stand-ards of the masses of the people.[4]

Because of the stress on import-substitution using capital-intensive measures, insufficient industrial employment was generated, and most of the burden was borne by agriculture. The primary sector, mainly agriculture, which had employed an estimated 75 per cent of the population producing 54 per cent of national income at the end of British rule,[5] was still, by 1991, employing 67 per cent of the workforce, but its share of GDP had come down to 31 per cent meaning in effect that nearly as many in agriculture were getting a much smaller proportion of the total income.[6] This immiserated primary sector threw off its surplus labour, the large majority of them not getting well-protected jobs in factories but becoming the growing "unorganized sector" living in slums in cities and small towns.

In terms of human welfare this meant that the islands of growth in industry and agriculture did not result in significant welfare gains for the majority. The average lifespan rose to 58 for women and 60 for men by 1990, a significant gain from 44 and 46 respectively in 1965 and from the drastic situation of the colonial period when life expectancy did not reach 30 until 1941. But it was a stunted and undernourished population surviving on an average of only 2229 calories per day,[7] and India remains the only major country in the world where women continue to live shorter lives than men. Between 1980 and 1990, as an international survey on hunger showed, 41 per cent of children below four years of age were classified as underweight and 30 per cent of babies were born with low birth weights. 20 per cent of the population even in the 1980s were without access to health facilities; 24 per cent of the urban and 50 per cent of the rural population were without access to safe water; and 28 per cent of urban and 40 per cent of the rural population were classified as below an absolute poverty level.[8] By the World Bank's figures, in absolute numbers there were 420 million poor and 250 million "extremely poor"; of the poor, 77 per cent were estimated to be rural.[9] This was, according to the Bank, a decline since 1972, but sheer numbers still made India the largest poor country in the world, housing over one-third of the world's poor.

This was a far cry from the dreams both of India's freedom fighters, who had fought not only for independence but also for prosperity and equality, and of the dalit and non-brahman critics who had insisted above all on equality. Today, whether or not the new economic policies will actually succeed in their professed goals, whether inequalitarian capitalism or a more sustainable development will follow, the pressure for liberalization comes more from the failures of this earlier statist regime, the Nehruvian model, than from influences exerted by imperialist institutions.

How much was this stagnant, bureaucratically top-heavy, impoverished form of development related to a caste system in which (according to the later Mandal Commission report) the public sector continued to be brahman-dominated, i.e. with 15 percent "forward castes" holding nearly 70 per cent of all positions and 90 per cent of Class I positions? There has been, strikingly, little effort to join an analysis of the specific nature of India's developmental path to a critique of the caste system as a crucial part of its social structure.

A recent attempt has been made by a liberal economist, Deepak Lal, who argues in *The Hindu Equilibrium* that the caste system represented a form of labour organization that led to a stagnant but relatively high level of living standards by pre-capitalist norms, with a "predatory state" or "revenue state" living mainly off the surplus from agriculture. The most oppressive feature of British rule, according to Lal, lay not in any positive blocking of development but in failing to break through this equilibrium. With independence and a mainly brahmanic elite inheriting the hoary bureaucracy, the "casteist revenue economy" got "a new lease of life in the modern ideological garb of fabian socialism".[10] Lal thus connects brahmanism, the caste system, the hostility to a market economy and preference for a bureaucratically-controlled command economy with slow growth in both agriculture and industry. In a sense, (to use more Marxist language) in

69

seeing the main contradiction of the colonial period as with caste-feudalism rather than imperialism, many aspects of this argument resonate with the political positions argued by Phule, Periyar and Ambedkar.

Equally striking has been a recent article in the *Economic and Political Weekly* by B.P.R Vithal on "the roots of Hindu fundamentalism," arguing that in fact Hindu traditions could be sustained only with a growth rate of between 0 and 3 per cent and "if we get on to a trajectory of a consistently faster rate of growth (and) it merely succeeds in breaking present moulds there will be a rootlessness which can be dangerous in a large country like ours."[11] M. Shivaiah has argued from a dalit perspective, that this position amounts to a justification for an alliance with the BJP and that Vithal, a high-level IAS official, represents a widespread trend in the bureaucracy.[12]

Along with linkages of brahmanism and bureaucraticization, we can argue that the general orientation to an idealistic, abstract intellectualism (a socialism which conceives that slogans of *garibi hatao* are the equivalent of eradicating poverty, that passing laws and schemes is sufficient, that solving a problem theoretically is the equivalent of solving it empirically) can be called a characteristic of brahmanism. These are all highly contentious issues, but they do suggest that breaking through the high-caste monopoly of political and administrative positions, along with breaking the hold of the bureaucracy and political structure on the economy itself (not to be confused with establishing a positive welfare, infrastructural and guiding role for the state), is a necessary condition for achieving a healthy economic growth.

In any event, whatever position we may take in the debate about causes, the problems of economic stagnation, mass marginalization, immiseration of the majority of those connected with agriculture and traditional artisan manufactures, are very real ones. They are not simply the problems

70

of the 1980s. By the mid 1960s, after the first flush of independence had passed, the developmental effort was moving into crisis, with stagnation on both industrial and agricultural fronts. With food imports and U.S. pressure it was becoming clear that this path of development could not achieve even the self-reliance it promised. New upsurges of workers, peasants and agricultural labourers began, the Naxalite revolt in 1967 seemed to signal a new era of revolution, and from the early 1970s, spearheaded by the militant Dalit Panthers of Maharashtra, new social movements emerged on the Indian political arena. Their challenge to the system of exploitation was also beginning to be more and more a challenge to the Hindu-dominant symbolism of Indian identity.

9

Hinduism as Feudal Backwardness: The Dalit Panthers

The present Congress rule is essentially a continuation of the old Hindu feudalism which kept the dalits deprived of power, wealth and status for thousands of years ... the entire state machinery is dominated by the feudal interests, who for thousands of years, under religious sanctions, controlled all the wealth and power, who today own most of the agricultural land industry, economic resources and all other instruments of power....

Who is a dalit? Members of scheduled castes and tribes, neo-Buddhists, the working people, the landless and poor peasants, women and all those who are being exploited politically, economically and in the name of religion.

Who are our friends? Revolutionary parties set to break down the caste system and class rule. Left parties that are left in a true sense. All other sections of society that are suffering due to economic and political oppression.

Who are our enemies? Power, wealth, price. Landlords, capitalists, moneylenders and their lackeys.

Those parties who indulge in religious or casteist politics and the government which depends on them...
We do not want a little place in Brahman Alley.
We want the rule of the whole land. We are not looking at persons but a system. Change of heart, liberal
education, etc. will not end our state of exploitation.
When we gather a revolutionary mass, rouse the
people, out of the struggle of this giant mass will
come the tidal wave of revolution.[1]

This quote is from the manifesto of the Dalit Panthers, a
militant organization of dalit youth. Born in Bombay in 1972,
with its leadership drawn from a new generation of young
poets and writers, and founded against the backdrop of increasing rural and urban tensions—it was a period in which
atrocities against dalits in the villages, often of brutal and
horrifying forms, seemed on the increase—the Dalit Panthers
proved to be the spark that set off a wave of organizing
efforts throughout the country. In Karnataka, a dispute over
a cultural issue (a dalit minister was forced to resign after
describing conventional Kannada literature as "cattle feed")
led to widespread clashes throughout the state between
dalits and caste Hindus. The dalits raised the slogan, "Throw
the brahmans into the gutter along with the Gita" and eventually formed the Dalit Sangarsh Samiti with branches all
over the statè. In Bihar, a revived Naxalite movement sprang
up among the dalits, with issues of honour or *izzat* (mainly
the protection of dalit women against landlord molestation)
and agricultural wages being central. In Tamil Nadu,
Ambedkarite organizations began to be founded in many
villages. Other areas were slower to pick up the cue: a Dalit
Panther unit was formed in Gujarat in 1980 after widespread
upper-caste rioting in protest against reservations; an Andhra Dalit Mahasabha was formed in 1984 after a brutal mas-
sacre of dalits in the village of Karamchedu. Whatever its

form in each region, a new movement was enveloping most of the country, and the question "will the caste war turn into a class war?" almost began to replace the more conventional, "will the Green Revolution turn into a red one?"

Individual efforts were also underway to give a new theoretical articulation to the class-caste struggle. This question was taken up by V.T. Rajshekar of Bangalore, the founder-editor of *Dalit Voice* and though he swung fairly quickly to an emphasis almost solely on caste struggle, his articulate, aggressive and often vitriolic journalism won him readers throughout the country and among dalits abroad. A more Marxist attempt at integration was made by Sharad Patil, a district organizer of the CPI(M) in the tribal belt of Maharashtra. He took time off from his party work to study Sanskrit as a basis for a theoretical interpretation of Indian history, produced a new approach, "Marxism-Phule-Ambedkarism" and then a new party, the Satyashodhak Communist Party. In Andhra, Kancha Ilaiah of the Naxalite tradition began to theorize the role of both patriarchy and caste. Theory almost inevitably led to political action. Though the Panthers themselves were born in the context of a great disillusionment with the traditional Ambedkarite Republican Party, and even leaped to fame with an electoral boycott in 1974 that significantly benefited the communist candidate in the heart of Bombay's working class area, the thrust of the movement took them into electoral as well as revolutionary politics. One of the most important of the new parties was founded by a Punjabi dalit, Kanshi Ram, who had been turned into an Ambedkarite after his experiences in Maharashtra. Kanshi Ram avoided the Panthers and the more flashy dalit agitations of the time, and began with an organization of dalit, backward caste and minority government employees. He developed this by 1980 into the Bahujan Samaj Party, with its base mainly in north and north-west India and an ability to cut drastically into the taken-for-granted "vote banks" of the Congress. Another was the Bharatiya Republican Party, founded at almost the same time by Prakash Ambedkar, the grandson of Dr. Ambedkar. With the Buddhist revival, and a wave of conversions to Islam that was overplayed by the Hindutva forces to stress a "danger to Hinduism", the new ferment was clearly covering all aspects of social life.

The Panthers had been the starting point of this ferment and their thrust was to universalize the dalit identity as proletarian experience. This differentiated it from the dalit movement of Ambedkar's time, which had accepted the separation of economic and cultural spheres, of class and caste, sometimes ignoring the economic sphere substantially. It also contrasted with the first new left upsurge in India, the Naxalite revolt, with its rural orientation and Maoist fervour for agrarian revolution. Now, after the Naxalites had been crushed (at least temporarily) in Bombay, the bastion of Indian capitalism itself, economic exploitation and cultural oppression intertwined to define a new dalit revolt—linked in imagery if not in terms of a concrete socio-economic analysis.

Many factors brought about the Dalit Panther phenomenon: the economic crisis which had been unfolding since the middle 1960s, the disillusionment with the history of corruption and co-opting of the party founded by Ambedkar; the spread of education; and the nature of the capitalist city as a communications centre. It is true, of course to say that the poets and activists of the dalit movement were "petty bourgeois" or "middle class"; but what was striking was the changing nature of this middle class and its increased spread. In Ambedkar's time this consisted of only a very small section of educated dalits who could provide the core of activists for a movement; by the 1970s education and the gains from reservations had produced a widespread section. It ranged upwards to a few high-level government employees and political leaders and downwards to the villages, where in most areas some minimal education of the boys of the most conscious dalit castes (Mahars, Chambhars, etc.) was practically universal and was slowly beginning to include the girls as well. The nature of the Indian education system made them vulnerable to the modernistic upgradings of Hindu ideologies found in school books; but simultaneously the ability to read and write proved a powerful weapon for the movement.

Both education, whatever its limitations, and the communications network of the time made a range of contemporary and historical world events a reality for an increasing number of the poor themselves. The Vietnam revolution, the Chinese revolution, the Black movement and Black poetry, Marxism, the women's movement, the new left, were all part of the cultural mix that represented a world-wide phenomenon. In describing Bombay from its red light districts to its mixed culture and language, the images of Namdev Dhasal, greatest of the early dalit poets and a Panther founder, show a stretch in time, from the crystalized images of India's past to the age of revolutions. They show the consciousness born out of a classic industrialized world juxtaposed with the miseries of village immigrants whose ignorance was symbolized in the mother:

> In the eighteenth century the whole human race was
>   turned upside down,
> but even today you haven't heard of it...
> Mother, your son is not a child.
> He is the son of this age's rebellion,
> he can see clearly the injustice, himself as victim,
> governmental machinery, means of living, power of toil,
>   mines of coal and steel, warehouses, factories,
> there: protection, guarantee of food and money,
> my face, lying in the dust, separated from all of this.[2]

The early dalit upsurge had a strong Naxalite flavour; dalits identified themselves as modern and proletarian and saw their enemy—Hinduism—as feudal backwardness. Militancy was a crucial aspect of this. As a dalit activist of the Bombay slums recalled the period, "We knew nothing of what was written in the Manifesto. All we knew was that if someone put his hand on your sister—cut if off!" This near nihilist mood and fierce anger distinguished it from early twentieth century movements and made the Dalit Panthers specifically and the whole new dalit movement generally, an aspect of a worldwide "new left" upsurge. Indeed, it was at this time that the term"'dalit" or downtrodden, the 1930s' and 1940s' Marathi/Hindi translation of this British category of "Depressed Classes," became widespread: a militant alternative to the Gandhian term "Harijan" and the colourless governmental "Scheduled Castes"

The combining of economic and cultural radicalism was also common to many new left movements of the period. Whereas the traditional Indian left, including the Naxalites, during almost this entire period scarcely spoke of cultural issues or critiqued Hinduism as such, for the young dalit poets, economic and cultural exploitation were interwoven from the beginning. The Manifesto (written under a pronounced Naxalite ideological influence), after condemning Hinduism as feudalism, had really nothing to say about caste issues; the poetry however spoke of caste, of Buddha, of brahmans, of Shambuk and Ekalavya just as it spoke of poverty and the meaninglessness of parliamentary democracy. It ranged over all of Indian history and mythology, claiming a new past as well as laying claim to the future. For the poets it was as important to curse both god and the modern university as it was to expose capitalism—

One day I cursed that mother-fucker god
He just laughed shamelessly.

77

My neighbour, a born-to-the-pen Brahman, was shocked.
He looked at me with his castor-oil face...
I cursed another good hot curse
The university buildings shuddered and sank waste-deep.
All at once scholars began doing research
into what makes people angry...[3]

Their modernism was turned against the caste system, as much as it was turned against economic exploitation:

I stand today at the very end
of the twentieth century.
All around me is in flame...
Taking in one hand the sun, in the other the moon,
I am conscious of my resolve,
the worth of the blood of Ekalavya's broken finger.[4]

Marxism, as known in India, had separated class and caste oppressions; now the two were sought to be joined. This new project laid the ground for the upsurges of the 1970s and 1980s. The Panthers, in fact, rose and fell like a flash. Their first split came within only two years, rhetorically structured on the lines of "Buddhism versus Marxism Raja Dhale, leader of the Buddhist faction, claimed that his opponent Namdev Dhasal was a tool in the hands of the Marxists. Much of the intense dalit debate at this time took place at a seemingly crude level ("Who is your father: Ambedkar or Marx?") but behind it lay a great fear of being controlled by articulate, sophisticated brahman radicals. And the leftists to a large degree laid themselves open to attack by their ignorance of the rules of the anti-caste discourse. (For example, the apparently trivial but symbolically important mistakes of spelling Phule's name as "Jyotiba" in the brahmanical fashion rather than "Jotiba" after the village deity continued to be made again and again by upper-caste communists).

Nevertheless, the fragmentation of the Panthers was only an episode in a long upsurge. Not only did dalits continue to organize and fight back but they also provided major themes of revolt to other new assertions of the time. If the proletarianization of dalit identity was a new universalism, a new claim to being a kind of vanguard it was also an effort to define the entire Indian revolution in terms of the upsurge of the low castes, the theme of "we are the proletariat" being expressed in numerous poems and constantly in speeches. It was typical, for instance, that the then Panther leader Arun Kamble, speaking of the Mandal Commission and the need for unity between dalits and non-brahmans at a Visham Nirmulan conference in the early 1980s, could argue for a "kunbi-ization" of Marathas (i.e. accepting their identity as toiling peasants rather than as "village rulers"), and end with the assertion: "We want dalitistan but not dalitistan as a separate country; we are 98.5%, we are the majority, *India shall become dalitistan*!" Dalits were, on such platforms, beginning to define identities and ideologies for other sections of the exploited.

The 1970s saw not only the rise of a new low-caste upsurge, but also the spread of a kind of "dalit consciousness" to many other movements. This came to signify the uniting of social and economic issues. It was taken up for instance by A.K. Roy, an independent Marxist leader of mine workers and the Jharkhand movement. In a pamphlet called "The New Dalit Revolution" published in 1980, Roy attacked the entire upper-caste leadership of left movements, attempted to theorize the geographical/social basis of Indian hierarchy in terms of the interaction between a hilly tribal area, a river bank-centered feudal civilization, and a port city-centered colonial civilization. Roy called for a fresh "discovery of India" through the participation of intellectuals in movements.

Whether the Indian bourgeoisie is black or white, big

or small has very little bearing on the politics of the country. What really matters are two basic features: caste system with uneven development of history and its interaction with the belated capitalism percolating from the top...

The communists have prepared various blueprints of revolution like National Democratic Revolution, Peoples' Democratic Revolution, New Democratic Revolution, and many other forms using mysterious terms hardly understood or even remembered by their own followers, not to speak of the toiling millions at large, while India needs a simple New Dalit Revolution, a policy of red and green flag combining the struggles for social emancipation with that against economic exploitation to storm the citadel of colonialism in the country.

Roy went on to assert the need for a cultural revolution within the Indian left, insisting that the symbols of the people should not be Rama or Krishna but those of the low-caste masses—often local, tribal and peasant leaders such as Birsa Munda (leader of an adivasi revolt in the nineteenth century), or Veer Narayan Singh (the adivasi chieftain who fought Aurangzeb):

The culture of the people, struggle of the oppressed like that of Birsa Munda of Chotanagpur and Veer Narayan Singh of Chattisgarh would be highlighted which is now obscured and would be restored to its rightful place above the wars and conspiracies of the feudal kings and colonial rulers which now crowd the pages of history From Buddha to Lenin it would be a unique journey, a new search for a spirit of emancipating millions, *a new religion not only a new party*, out to make a new history for mankind without exploitation, subjugation and with justice.[5]

10

The Logic of Dalit Politics

The "unique journey" that A.K. Roy had called for seemed to be beginning in the 1970s. Numerous youth went to the villages, new activists rose from the masses, social turmoil increased as economic and social pressures mounted, and new voices rose as other low-caste and oppressed sections joined dalits in organizing.

Dalit themes were expressed also by tribals, for instance Waharu Sonavane, an adivasi poet-activist coming out of a Marxist-led movement of Bhil agricultural labourers and poor peasants of northera Maharashtra. He was an activist sensitive from the beginning to cultural issues but by the late 1980s these were becoming dominant themes, as he challenged the control of non-tribals in adivasi-based movements. He began to argue that the adivasis who had been fragmented by religious identity and political parties should come together. But while he was willing to include BJP adivasi politicians in this coming together, Waharu clearly identified with the heritage of *rakshasas,* dismissing Rama as an exploiter and giving a unique adivasi perspective on the entire non-Aryan theme.

A strong alliance between minority of brahmans and a handful of rajas took one after the other adivasi tribes

81

under their control through violence and aggression. They made them into slaves and disarmed toiling peasants paying taxes to rajas, and settled them in villages to enlarge their kingdoms through settled agriculture. Between the sixth century B.C., that is the period of Buddha, and the fifth centuries A.D. a defined caste hierarchy and jajmani system was established. Most free adivasi tribes became toiling castes giving surplus to rajas and brahman-dominated feudal society! This society had the capacity to slowly transform adivasi tribes and absorb them in the hierarchy, but at lower levels. *We were those who faced this but remained free....* . When the adivasis of that time began to resist the atrocities against them, the Aryans became enraged. Then the Aryans went to the ruler of that time, their raja Shri Ramachandra, with the demand 'protect us from the rakshasas, our herds need open fields.' Rama gave a promise. Under the leadership of Ramchandraji adivasis of that time were slaughtered as rakshasas and crushed.[1]

Later, in the 1990s, Waharu joined with other adivasis of Maharashtra, Gujarat, Rajasthan and Madhya Pradesh in organizing Adivasi Ekta, a strongly autonomous organization of tribals.

The 1980s were marked not only by the assertion of dalits and other low castes, but also by the rise of other new social movements, of farmers fighting against their exploitation by the market and state, of women, of tribal and caste Hindu peasants fighting against environmental destruction and displacement. These movements began to identify at least in part—at the beginning—with a critique of Hinduism and to put forward new cultural themes that began to converge with those of the dalit and anti-caste movement. Sometimes they drew consciously on this tradition.

In the new post-1975 women's movement, for example, there was initially a strong rejection by feminists of religion as such, with the underlying theme that "all religions are patriarchal and oppress women" replacing the pre-independence tendency to take Sita and Savitri as ideals of womanhood. For some time, this religious-cultural critique remained at an abstract level; then in the late 1980s, partly under the impact of the rise of fundamentalism, many women activists began to look for aspects of their own tradition that they could identify with. For some this meant a clear identification with Hinduism. Madhu Kishwar of the well-known women's magazine *Manushi* attacked only the militaristic and aggressive depiction of Rama by fundamentalists but upheld an ideal Ram. Other feminists looked for what some called "even more fundamental" religious traditions: at the role played by *devis* or goddesses in Indian tradition, the co-opting of that role, and ways it might be recovered. In the words of a song by Kamla Bhasin,

> *Every woman in this country is dishonoured, degraded,*
> *With your hand on your heart, say, how can such a country*
> *   be free?*
> *In this country, they say, there are goddesses without*
> *   number,*
> *Tell me, have they loosened even a link of our chains?*
> *Have we gained anything of honour from the veil?*
> *Beneath the veil we have remained smothered, beneath the*
> *   veil we burned...*
> *make the veil into a flag, unfurl it everywhere,*
> *We will bring humanity's rule to this land.*
> *You will not be able to challenge the power of women now!*
> *We are resolved to take on even the form of Kali Mata.*

By late 1980s dalit and other low-caste women, and feminists from south India were also making themselves heard. They tried to recover non-Aryan and anti-brahman traditions, took Sita as a symbol of oppression rather than an ideal, and argued that the Ramayana represented the triumph of patriarchy over matriarchy. Ruth Manorama, a dalit Christian from Bangalore involved in organizing slum dwellers, began to speak of the "triply oppressed", focusing on brahmanism as a major factor in women's oppression but not sparing dalit men either. She and others eventually organized the National federation of Dalit Women. At the 1991 National Women's Studies Conference in Calcutta two minority feminists, Flavia Agnes and Razia Patel, were openly attacking "Hindu hegemony" in the women's movement.

The environmental movement also saw a similar development, the emergence of culturally radical themes contesting a dominant trend that identified, though more ambiguously than in the colonial period, with a reformist Hinduism. Middle-class environmentalism had been Gandhian in inspiration, mounting a strong ideological attack on industrial civilization and "western science and technology" that included a tendency to idealize Indian traditional culture. This even involved some indifference to or even idealization of caste, with the most important academic study of the "ecological history of India" giving what was in effect a functionalist justification of caste as a system of ecological adaption.[2] Ecofeminists like Vandana Shiva emphasized the mother-goddess theme in women's writing as the protector of nature and identifyed it with "Prakriti"[3] However environmental mass movements based on peasants and other low castes very often used more anti-Brahman traditions. Thus a movement for water rights on the river Ganga used the symbol of Ekalavya, with the fishing communities they organized identifying themselves with this tribal hero of the epic. In southern Maharashtra, a strong local farmers' struggle for a peasant-built small dam identified itself with the tradition of Phule and named it the Bali Raja Memorial Dam.

Bali Raja became an important symbol for other mass movements in Maharashtra as well. A group working among other backward castes in the Vidarbha region took it as a major theme of yearly celebrations, and it became also a central symbol for the most powerful mass movement in the state, the Shetkari Sanghatna. its leader, Sharad Joshi, though himself a brahman, used the symbols of the people to explicate his "Bharat versus India" contradiction in society between the (mainly urban) exploiting sections and the (mainly rural) exploited. Gandhian models were evoked to stress that village and agriculture-centered development had to be followed rather than one based on state-controlled industry—this was no longer Ram Raj but Bali's kingdom, and the 1989 Nanded conference of the Shetkari Sanghatana took the popular peasant saying but turned it into an affirmative "troubles and sorrows *will go*, the kingdom of Bali *will come*." The Karnataka Rayat Sangh, another strong regional farmers' movement, used anti-caste themes from a Lohiaite tradition and tried to make alliances with the dalit movement in Karnataka. On the other hand, leaders of the farmers' movement in the Hindi belt, such as the Jat leader Mahendra Singh Tikait, spoke an anti-brahmanic language but identified with the more orthodox versions of Hinduism popular there.

There was thus an extreme unevenness in the culture of popular movements of the 1980s: a spread of the challenge to orthodox Hindu traditions, but marked at points with what was from the dalit point of view, a compromise with brahmanism on the part of some sections, and at others with a readiness to identify with other religious and cultural fundamentalisms as a counter to brahmanic Hinduism. These counter-fundametalisms were perhaps strongest in the complex movements arising in the peripheral nationalities. In Punjab, opposition to brahman-bania Delhi rule involved an identification with Sikh religious traditions that at points turned into a strong fundamentalism, including efforts to regulate women's dress and suppression of intellectual inquiry. In Kashmir, Islamic and socialist tendencies were mixed in a guerrilla armed struggle against the centre, and fundamentalist Islamist trends took over when the more secular forces were crushed by the Indian state after 1981. In Assam, much of the movement from 1980 onwards seemed to be dominated by high-caste Hindu students. The more militant armed struggle group, the United Liberation Front of Assam, the ULFA, on the other hand, picked up the theme of northeastern uniqueness: their Assam, never conquered by Hindus or Muslims, was very largely "Mongoloid, Tibeto-Mongoloid, and Austric" in contrast to the Aryan-Dravidian mainland, as their petition before the General Assembly of the UN put it.

Thus, in many ways the 1980s saw, below the surface of the growth of Hindutva and Congress corruption, complex processes of cultural dialogue. Compared to the colonial period, there was intense interaction between the various forms of opposition to the Indian state, with the left forces also involved in various ways. Yet the period was still marked by ongoing contradictions and a failure to evolve a total liberatory theory.

The logic of dalit politics, it may be argued, involved three major emerging themes:

- a challenge to the very definition of Hinduism as the majority religion and the core of Indian tradition; an insistence that it was rather a brahmanic Hinduism that represented the hegemony of an elite over that tradition, and that this hegemony had to be overthrown;
- a spreading of this theme beyond dalits themselves to involve all the sections of the oppressed, exploited and marginalized by the processes of caste exploitation, including adivasis and other backward castes (the former shudras), peasants, women, and oppressed nationalities; and

- a synthesis of a new economic and political direction with the cultural challenge.

For dalit politics to succeed, it may be argued, all of these were necessary. And the story of the 1980s and 1990s was in large part a failure to achieve this.

The 1980s and 1990s saw the fading of the Congress as the dominant hegemonic party in India, in spite of a temporarily renewed sympathy vote after the assassination of Indira Gandhi, in spite of the "clean" technologically oriented initial liberalization represented by her son Rajiv Gandhi. Instead, alternatives were in the air. At first it appeared that a new political force could arise from a base in the new social movements to come as an alternative. This was the V.P. Singh-led National Front government, its core the newly formed socialist Janata Dal. All of the new movements, from Dalits to farmers to environmentalists, backed it; Datta Samant, the militant unorthodox working class leader, and Sharad Joshi, the most articulate of the new farmers' leader, joined in the campaign. Yet though V.P. Singh came to power as Prime Minister, his government lasted only a short eleven months. His announcement of the implementation of the Mandal Commission report—caste reservations for "other backward classes," that is, the former Shudra castes—provoked a strong reaction. Agitations broke out among the upper castes, with the attempt at suicide by burning by a young student provoking numerous others, many of whom succeeded. This was followed in October 1990 by a "rath yatra" campaign of Hindutva forces, now organized under the Bharatiya Janata Party, led by Lal Krishna Advani, aimed at constructing a Hindu temple in Ayodhya. This time, on 6 December, the mosque at Ayodhya, the "Babri Masjid," named after Babar, the original Mughal conqueror of India, was smashed and demolished, and hundreds of people died in the rioting that followed. Anti-Muslim sentiment surged. Fanatical pro-leaders like Bal Thackeray of Maharashtra's Shiv Sena said openly to *Time* magazine that, "have (Indian Muslims) behaved like the Jews in Nazi Germany? If so, there is nothing wrong if they are treated as Jews were in Nazi Germany... In politics we follow Shivaji. In religion it's Shiva. The third eye is now opening."[4] No one dared arrest him at the time. The V.P. Singh government fell, to be replaced briefly by a caretaker government led by Chandrasekhar, and then the Congress returned to power, following the horrifying assassination of Rajiv Gandhi, on a sympathy vote under the leadership of the old Congress politician, Narsimha Rao.

Dalits themselves in the meantime had organized a political party, one which was to prove more lasting than the amorphous third front of V.P. Singh. In the late 1970s a young Dalit government defence employee, Kanshi Ram, had quit his job in Pune to organize BAMCEF–the "Backward and Minority Communities Employees' Federation," a coalition of all groups oppressed by caste. This was the first time a dalit had taken up the task of organizing the "OBCs," the ex-Shudras. Kanshi Ram from the beginning had what appeared to be grandiose ideas, and when he began to form political fronts and take part in election campaigns, primarily in the north where the largest dalit community, the Chamars, had a widespread presence, no one at first took notice. The organization of the Bahujan Samaj Party (BSP) went unremarked by most left and progressive forces, largely because it appeared to have no other goal than to win political power.

In fact, while Kanshi Ram assiduously avoided adopting an economic programme, he had a clear social agenda: destroy the BSO, the "Brahmanical Social Order." He began to popularize the "four pillars" of the anti-caste movement in north India and elsewhere—Phule, Ambedkar, Periyar and Shahu Maharaj. Dalit politicians working with the Congress were condemned as *chamchas* (spoons, i.e. puppets, a common Indian phrasing). Kanshi Ram instead wanted to unite all dalits and ex-shudras under the category of *bahujan* and organize them for the sole goal of achieving political power. "We must become a ruling community," was the slogan of Ambedkar most frequently remembered. All of this was backed up by energetic organizing, numerous "awareness campaigns," cycle tours and rallies. Then he picked up a young woman ICS officer, Mayavati, herself a *chamar*, and began projecting her as a political leader.

By the elections of 1989 and 1991 the BSP was gaining some significant victories, and in 1993 it came to power in U.P. in an alliance with Mulayam Singh Yadav's Samajwadi Party—a party mainly based on OBCs, especially the aspirant *yadavas* or cowherds. Mayavati became the first truly autonomous dalit chief minister in India—a woman at that. Kanshi Ram turned UP over to her and began touring the south, where the BSP was picking up new cadres everywhere, many ex-Naxalites and leftists disillusioned with the traditional left and motivated by its daring. But in UP, the alliance proved short-lived. Political competitors and later personal enemies in the violence-ridden politics of UP, there was a falling out between Mulayam and Mayavati. The SP withdrew its support, and the first BSP government fell. This rift between a mainly OBC party and the still mainly Dalit BSP, along with the continuing decline of the Congress, left UP politics in a turmoil. However, two more BSP governments were to come, minority regimes headed by Mayawati—only now taking the support of the BJP, an implicit alliance that left many sympathizers very unhappy.

The truly emergent new hegemonic political force proved to be the party of "Hindu nationalism," the Bharatiya Janata Party. Backed by the organized, militant force of the Rashtriya Swayamsevak Sangh (RSS), and with numerous offshoots—women's organizations, fanatic youth squads such as the Bajrang Dal, the militant Vishwa Hindu Parishad—it now made a concerted drive for power. By the late 1990s, it was in the process of overcoming the Congress as the hegemonic political party, ruling India with a group of motley allies in the National Democratic Alliance (NDA). The Congress, struggling to regain its position, could only turn again to the Nehru dynasty for leadership—Rajiv's Italian-born widow Sonia, and then their children, Priyanka and Rahul.

Dalits had always mistrusted both parties, and seen Gandhism as only a more seemingly progressive version of Hindutva: after all, massive and horrifying anti-Muslim riots in Gujarat, the centre of Gandhi's influence, seemed to prove that the Hindutva Ram Raj was only a step removed from Gandhi's Ram Raj.

Baburao Bagul, an award-winning writer and one-time Communist party member, had written condemning the hegemony of Hindu themes in the national movement. He argued that in Europe, nationalism and the bourgeois revolution had a progressive content and people had fought religious authority, but in India nationalism "was turned into a form of ancestor worship". Bagul went on to argue that, since "Hindus are the majority," there was little to hope for from the Indian tradition:

Democratic socialism which is based on liberty, equality and fraternity is the philosophy of the modern age. And this philosophy has no roots in the Indian psyche and mystical value-structure. The literature of the saints has not provided any valuable alternative in the forms of ideals. On the other hand, fascism, *varna*-domination, hero-worship, pride, scorn, malice and hatred—all these have solid literary and intellectual support.[5]

A young poet, Vilas Rashinikar, put it equally strongly:

From pitch black tunnels
they gather ashes
floating on jet-black water
and reconstruct the skeletons

of their ancestors,
singing hymns
of their thoughts
worn to shreds.
There is no entry here
for the new sun.
This is the empire
of ancestor-worship,
of blackened castoffs,
of darkness.[6]

Dalit politics, thus, made important strides in the 1980s
and 1990s. For most it was indeed a major alternative to the
rise of Hindutva. But the failure to evolve a broader vision
which could make it a leader of a mass upsurge continued to
hamper its development.

11

Conclusion: Sita's Curse, Shambuk's Silence

There is an overwhelming consensus among scholars and journalists (not to speak of a large section of common people) that India is a nation of Hindus (or a Hindu majority nation), and that the main fight is between communalists and secularists over its definition. Yet, this consensus is based on surprisingly thin logic. Take, for instance, this passage from an *Economist* article on "The Hindu Upsurge":

> What is a Hindu? The answer is surprisingly complex. Thousands of years ago, Aryans from Central Asia migrated to the Indian subcontinent, conquering the local tribes. The holy books of the Aryans, the Vedas, were a mixture of philosophy, prayers and stories about their many gods. As the Aryans mingled with the original inhabitants, many local beliefs and further gods joined the Vedic ones. This loose conglomeration of deities and beliefs came to be called Hinduism. The word originally referred to people living around the Indus river. It has always denoted a society rather than a faith, let alone a church.... [1]

This is an apparently objective account; but it does not

mention that the subcontinent contained not simply "tribes" but also a civilization, and takes "Aryan" as the foundation element to which other religious themes are added. Yet, in repeating for us the theme that "Hindus" represent both a people and a set of beliefs (religion), it pinpoints a very clear dilemma. If Hinduism is a religion, then it cannot denote simply those living in the subcontinent, and as a religion (linked to brahmanism, a belief in the authority of the Vedas, and caste) it is not the original or national religion of the subcontinent. Many others (Buddhism, Jainism) can well claim to be older and still other religious definitions (Sikhism, Veerasaivism, tribal traditions) can legitimately claim to be outside the Hindu consensus. Hinduism, defined as a religion, cannot so easily claim majority status.

On the other hand, if Hinduism denotes a society—or a people living in a particular territory—then it can well claim cultural traditions reaching back to Mohenjo-daro and beyond, as well as encompass the diversity of races, ethnic groups and cultural particularities ranging from Kashmir to Kanyakumari, the north-east to the Rajasthan desert and beyond. But by this definition, which would include in the people all those incursions from outside the subcontinent as well (beginning with the Aryans and Dravidians themselves), there is no ground to exclude Indian Muslims and Indian Christians, to make any conditionalities upon their acceptance, or to take Rama, Krishna or any of the particular localized deities as definatory of a supposed national consensus. There is certainly no historical or logical ground to priorize a Vedic tradition. *This type of Hindu identity (which some would call Sindhu-Hindu on the grounds that Sindhu is after all the original pronunciation)*[2] *has clear equalitarian and antibrahmanic connotations.*

In other words, the construction of Hinduism as achieved by the Hindu-nationalists and accepted in various forms by many supposed secularists as well, rests on a trick:

conflating the two contradictory definitions of a broad, territorial, pluralistic, historical identity with a religious culture that continues to give dominance to an Aryan/Vedic/Sanskritic/ brahmanic core.

The *Economist* article goes on to say that the problem is not a Hindu-Muslim one but "an argument between secular and communal Hindus over the treatment of Muslims." But the issue is different and far deeper than this. The argument—the great cultural debate, the class/caste struggle—is over "what is Hindu" and "what is Indian," and it is, in the end, between the upholders of a brahmanic, patriarchal tradition and the exploited low-caste masses.

This is where the Aryan issue becomes significant. Phule had propounded the theory of the Aryan invasion as the source of oppression; dalit radicals of the 1920s took it to its extreme; Ambedkar denied it. The crude version of this dalit anti-Aryanism, as scholars are quick to point out, is fallacious as well as a form of inverted racism: there is no real evidence that the Aryans were responsible for destroying the Indus valley civilization, and tracing the caste system solely to events of conquest is inadequate.[2] Yet the imagery survives and for good reasons. The continual privileging of an Aryan identity and a Vedic-Upanishadic-Sanskritic core by almost all upper-caste definers of Indian tradition, the pride in being "white" in opposition to "black," the continual assumptions of northern superiority, the continual if always veiled forms of upper-caste arrogance: all of these make it almost inevitable that the angry dalit-shudra masses will throw back the weapon of racial and ethnic identity and ask again, "Who was the first invader? Who was the first outsider?"

The issue of brahmanism is as central as that of Aryanism. The attack on brahmanism can be theoretically differentiated from a rejection of the brahmans, yet one slides easily into another form of discourse on caste, feeding the already powerful fears of losing caste-linked privileges and power in a way that can become explosive—as the rioting and suicide wave following the announced implementation of the Mandal Commission report indicated. It is easy enough to point out that casteist prejudices and exclusiveness are pervasive at all levels of the hierarchy, that anti-brahmanism itself often takes racist forms, that merely attacking one section will not by itself provide an alternative for a humane society. Yet brahmanism seems clearly implicated. Militant anti-caste leaders such as Phule and Ambedkar, both of who had brahman colleagues, were quite rigorous about the conditions of their acceptance: for Phule, the Arya-bhats could be welcomed as long as they "threw away their bogus scriptures"; for Ambedkar, Hinduism could be saved if all the "Smrutis and Shastras" were given up.

This has been the simple demand of the anti-caste movement against the dominant elite. It has not happened; rather the issue has been evaded, either on secular grounds which claim that after all the solution must be political or economic (because it is the political use of religion which is producing the virus, or it is economic crisis which makes people turn in desperation to solutions of identity); or on reformist Hindu grounds which claim that the texts can be reinterpreted sufficiently to challenge the claims of the brahmans and shankaracharyas to represent them. In spite of the continuing simmering of the dalit, minority, anti-caste challenge from below, the face of India continues to be presented as a (brahmanic) Hindu one.

This leads many to despair and nihilism. For several militant dalits, as Bagul's essay shows, there is no hope in tradition; the Hindu majority (defined by brahmanism and Rama) is a solid one; the entire literature and mythology is pervaded with Brahmanism. Shudras and ati-shudras had been completely excluded from the literature, whether of the high or low tradition, and where they existed they illustrated

only the repressiveness of the system and its ability to pre-
vent or co-opt revolts against it. Bagul argues:

> The enemy had, of course, pervaded Indianness in its
> entirety; in traditions and customs, in the structure
> and system, in the books, words and minds.... . The
> caste system pervaded the life of the entire society.
> The intelligentsia were committed to religion...
> Hindu writers, therefore, find it difficult to cope with
> the Ambedkarite hero who is a rebel with a scientific
> and rationalist attitude; on the other hand, heroes like
> Karna and Ekalavya are consistent with the cultural
> and mythical value-structure they have internalised...
> (They) are reconciled to the *varna* system; they are
> courageous, but because they have been denied the
> place they deserve in the system, they view life only
> in terms of suffering; these heroes ... become simply
> toys in the hands of fate.[3]

Thus, Karna, Vidura, Ekalavya (the low-caste heroes in
the puranas) all in their different ways actually served the
brahmanical and feudal system in spite of their victimization
by it, and Shambuk, the shudra boy killed for the "sin" of
attempting to follow brahmanical yoga, is silent in the face
of the forces ranged against him, much as in a film on atrocities against tribals (*Aakrosh*), the tribal male hero is silent except for a cry of protest. Against this, the dalits could only
protest: while Ekalavya for example, was to be important for
them as an illustration of what *varnashrama dharma* meant,
they wanted him to do what the myths did not reveal him
doing, revolt:

> *If you had kept your thumb*
> *History would have happened*
> *somehow differently.*
> *But... you gave your thumb*

and history also
became theirs.
Ekalavya,
since that day they
have not even given you a glance.
Forgive me, Ekalavya, I won't be fooled now
by their sweet words.
My thumb
will never be broken.[4]

In the face of this apparently overwhelming oppressiveness of tradition, dalit radicals could only respond with a total negation:

You who have made the mistake of being born in this
    country
must now rectify it: either leave the country,
or make war![5]

But is Indian tradition totally oppressive? Is it necessary for either dalit or upper caste progressives who aspire to equality and liberation to reject Indian culture and identity totally? The whole point of the cultural critique from Jotiba Phule and Tarabai Shinde through Ambedkar, Periyar and others was to the contrary: their interpretations of Indian history and tradition rested not only on the negative exposure of caste hierarchy and domination but also on attempts to explore the rebellions and occasional triumphs of the low castes. And conversely, the problem with Nehruvian secularism in fighting a Hindu fundamentalism was not that it was secular and equalitarian, not that it asserted universal values of freedom and equality, but that in order to justify these it simply adopted without criticism the hegemonic, brahmanic interpretation of the tradition. Freedom and equality can in fact find their roots in tradition if that tradition is critically understood.

This requires a process of reinterpretation, because the voice of low castes, women, tribals, non-Aryans, etc. in myths was from the beginning filtered through the interpretations of their masters and conquerors. Shambuk was not silent, he was silenced; his voice was not recorded. Ekalavya may well have fought, but his fight has been erased from myths. In many cases though, the resistance was at least partially recorded, sometimes in the written versions of the legends and sometimes in folk versions that had to be recovered, searched out, and brought to a position of hegemony. These may seem obvious points, something that any social scientist and historian interpreting popular mythology knows: the document itself has been produced in a social process. It should not be necessary in these days of deconstructionism and post-modernism to point this out. But it has become necessary to repeat such points because even the academic interpretations of Indian culture, the ones most influenced by supposedly sophisticated methodologies, have very often taken the high-caste versions of the myths for granted, as texts which are taken to be the unexamined basis for theorizing.

Here the feminists attempting to unravel the complexities of Hindu patriarchal co-option have major contributions to offer the dalit contestation of Hinduism. The most interesting example of a suppressed, partly voiceless, seemingly co-opted heroine is Sita, the apparent paradigm of self-sacrificial devotion to a husband. In recent years she has been taken more often as the symbol of women's victimization. But there is much more to Sita than this, as even a reading of the Valmiki version of the Ramayana makes clear. Thus, we find her, for example, rebuking Rama in the name of the rakshasas:

> You are alarmingly close to that sinful state to which
> the ignorant are prone ... that is, killing a creature

who has not committed any offence.... O hero, my prayer is that when armed with the bow, you are engaged in waging war against the rakshasas, who have this forest for their home, you may never allow yourself to slay indiscriminately those who are not to blame.[6]

But Rama, in reply, makes it clear that his killing of the rakshasas, including the rakshasa queen Tataka, is out of a vow made to the brahmans of the Dandakaranya forest, and thus as part of a protection of caste hierarchy.

Even more important, beyond the Valmiki Ramayana, and its even more patriarchal successors (such as the Tulsidas Ramayana, which brought in the theme of the *lakshman rekha*) we find in Sita, inclinations to rebel. Some traditions depict her love for Ravana (indicating perhaps that this may be a subterranean theme of even the orthodox version in which she is only suspected:) There is a strong peasant-based tradition of Sita that emphasizes her rejection of Rama after she has been sent away, her anger at the injustices done to her. In a folk poem of Uttar Pradesh for instance, Sita refuses to go back even when Laxman has been sent to bring her, and instead raises her sons on her own and gives them her father's name, in a half-way return to matriliny. The Thai version of the Ramayana, similarly, ends with Sita refusing to go back until the gods themselves intervene to restore family propriety.[7]

One of the most interesting variations of the image of Sita comes from Maharashtra, the Sita of Raveri, and has been picked up by the Shetkari Sanghatana. Raveri is a small village in Yeotmal district where Sanghatna activists, in the process of a campaign to get peasants to put land in the names of the women of their family had come across an old, nearly abandoned Sita temple. "Rakshasas built it," say the villagers, and in fact the image is that of the typical village *devi*. In the story of Raveri, Sita after being forced to leave Ayodhya, wanders and settles in Raveri and because she has two small babies and cannot work, goes from house to house begging for flour. When the villagers refuse to give it (on the grounds that such an abandoned women must be a "bad woman") she curses that the village will not be able to grow wheat. Sure enough, say the villagers, they could not, until a few years back when hybrid varieties came in. Now, however, they are putting land in the name of women as a way of redressing the sins of their ancestors! There is also a Hanuman temple in the village with a more recently found "fallen Hanuman"—shot down by Sita's sons, people say, when he came to fetch her back.

Such versions where Sita is not simply a symbol of oppression but linked with *rakshasas* and identified with agriculture (but not "green revolution" agriculture), illustrates the real depth of all the counter depictions of the Ramayana: not as the story of Rama's triumph and the ideal family, but a story of his conquest over Dravidian and tribal native inhabitants, of the triumph of patriarchy over matriarchy, of the suppression of women connected with the establishment of a stable agricultural society (Sita is after all *bhumikanya* Sita, found below a furrow). It is ultimately a story which has many renditions in a long era of class/caste/gender struggle, of a conquest over a long time span, but also of the resistance and uniting of the conquered, a reversal, a forecasting of the liberation of peasants, dalits, women, and tribals.

The themes of caste domination, exploitation, and patriarchy come together, and Shambuk, Sita, Tataka, and Ravana are united in their victimization by the brahmanic Hindu system, and their rebellion against it. It is no longer possible to raise the image of Rama without confronting the totality of the story, and the debate is no longer being carried on simply by an upper-caste educated elite. The themes of

100

victimization and rebellion are themes that remain linked with the material life of the people, of peasants, women, dalits and tribals, and for that reason, threaten to burst forward even when the Hindutva attempt to hegemonize and crystallize the Ramayana as a symbol of Hindu orthodoxy seems closest to success. Reinterpretations and debates concerning the traditions of Gandhi and Nehru, as well as those of Ambedkar, Phule and Periyar will go on, but so different is the situation from the colonial period that Ram raj is no longer a viable ideal in India today any more than Nehruvian socialism.

Desperate beatings on the drums of an imagined uppercaste past will produce no longlasting victories. The evocation of the people's past will continue to have a role in the formulation of a new society, in which the major dalit theme remains that of confidence and aspiration, symbolized by numerous poems evoking a new sun, by the powerful call of the dalit balladeer Waman Kardak:

> *Chase away the army of darkness*
> *search the sky, the moon, the stars*
> *the light is in you*
> *the light is in you*
> *be tomorrow's sun.*[8]

Notes

NOTES TO CHAPTER 1

1. Sadashiv Bhave, "Bhakti in Modern Marathi Poetry," in Eleanor Zelliot and Maxine Berntsen, ed., *The Experience of Hinduism* (State University of New York Press, 1988), pp. 318-19.
2. Guna, *Asiatic mode: A Socio-Cultural Perspective* (Delhi: Bookwell Publications, 1984), pp. 124-25.

NOTES TO CHAPTER 2

1. See Rosalind O'Hanlon, *Caste, Conflict and Ideology; Mahatma Jotiba Phule and Low-Caste Social Protest in Nineteenth Century Western India* (Cambridge: Cambridge University Press, 1988) for an extended discussion of this.
2. See Gyanendra Pandey, "Hindus and others: The Militant Hindu Construction", *Economic and Political Weekly*, December 28, 1991 and Sitaram Yechury, "What is Hindu Rashtra? An Exposure of Golwalkar's Fascist Ideology and the Saffron Brigade's Practice", *Frontline*, March 12, 1993.
3. Pandey, *The Construction of Communalism in Colonial North India* (Delhi: Oxford University Press, 1990), p. 235.
4. See Gandhi's reply to Ambedkar's "Annihilation of Caste" in *The Harijan*, reprinted in *Dr. Babasaheb Ambedkar: Writings and Speeches*, Volume I (Bombay: Government of Maharashtra, 1979), p. 82.

5. *Ibid.*, p. 83.
6. See my study, *Dalits and the Democratic Revolution: Dr. Ambedkar and the Dalit Movement in Colonial India* (New Delhi: Sage, 1994), Chapter 5.
7. Ambedkar, from "Federation or Freedom," *op. cit.* p. 352.
8. Jawaharlal Nehru, *Towards Freedom: The Autobiography of Jawaharlal Nehru*, (John Day Co. 1941), pp. 410-11.
9. Jawaharlal Nehru, *The Discovery of India* (Oxford University Press, 1982), p. 138.
10. *Ibid.*, pp. 252-53.
11. Pandey, *The Construction of Communalism*, 253-54.

NOTES TO CHAPTER 3

1. Jotiba Phule,*Samagra Wanghmay* (Bombay:Government of Maharashtra, 1990), pp. 118-20.
2. See *Collected Works of Mahatma Jotirao Phule,* Volume II, Selections translated by P.G. Patil (Bombay: Government of Maharashtra, 1991), pp. 39-40.
3. *Ibid.*, p. 32.
4. See Uma Chakravarti, *Gender, Class and Nation; Ramabai and the Critique of Brahmanical Patriarchy* (forthcoming); "The Development of the Sita Myth: A Case Study", *Samya Shakti* I (1), July 1983; "Conceptualising Brahmanical Patriarchy in Early India: Gender, Class and State," *Economic and Political Weekly*, April 3, 1993; and "The Sita Who Refused the Fire Ordeal," *Manushi* No. 8, 1981.
5. From *Jotiba Phule: An Incomplete Renaissance, Seminar Papers* (Surat: Centre for Social Studies, 1991), "A summary of the Proceedings," page ix-x.
6. Phule, *Samagra Wangmay*, p. 440, translated by Gail Omvedt and Bharat Patankar.

NOTES TO CHAPTER 4

1. Phule, Samagra Wangmay, p. 372.

2. On Ramabai, see Chakravarti, *Gender, Class & Nation* and Meera Kosambi, "Indian Response to Christianity, Church and Colonialism: Case of Pandita Ramabai" *Economic and Political Weekly*, October 24-31, 1992.
3. Pandita Ramabai, *The High-Caste Hindu Woman* (Bombay: Government of Maharashtra, 1982; originally published 1887), p. 48.
4. *Ibid.*, p. 3.
5. *Ibid.*, p. 29.
6. Cited in Kosambi, "Indian Response to Christianity, Church and Colonialism," *Economic and Political Weekly* Women's Studies Supplement, October 24-31, 1992, p. 63.
7. Tarabai Shinde, *Stri-Purush Tulna* (Nagpur: Asoka Prakashan, 1992) (Marathi: my translation).
8. *Ibid.*, p. 6.
9. *Ibid.*, p. 8.
10. Partha Chatterjee, "The Nationalist Resolution of the Women's Question," in Kumkum Sangari and Sudesh Vaid, *Recasting Women: Essays in Colonial History* (Delhi: Kali for Women Press, 1989). p. 238.
11. See the discussions in Jana Everett, *Women and Social Change in India* (New Delhi: Heritage, 1981).
12. Kapil Kumar, "Rural Women in Oudh, 1917- 1947," in Sangari and Vaid, *Recasting Women*, p. 351.
13. *Ibid.*, p. 363 (quote from an interview with Jaggi).
14. Sumanta Banerjee, "Women's Popular Culture in Nineteenth Century Bengal," in *Ibid.* pp. 138-39.

NOTES TO CHAPTER 5

1. Quoted in M.E. Bhagwat, "Vidarbhatil Dalit Vicharanci Netrutva", in P.L. Joshi, ed., *Political Ideas and Leadership in Vidarbha* (Nagpur, 1980), p. 297.
2. See Omvedt, *Dalits and the Democratic Revolution*, Chapter 3.
3. Cited in M.G. Gautam, "The Untouchables' Movement in Andhra Pradesh," *Andhra Pradesh State Harijan Souvenir*, (Hyderabad; Government Press, 1976), p. 67.
4. *Census of India, 1931, Volume XXIII, Hyderabad State; Part I: Report* (Hyderabad-Deccan; Government Central Press, 1933), p. 258.
5. Quoted in R.S. Khare, *The Untouchable as Himself: Ideology,*

Identity and Pragmatism Among the Lucknow Chamars (London: Cambridge University Press, 1984).p. 85. See also Owen Lynch, *The Politics of Untouchability* (New York: Columbia University Press, 1969).

6. Quoted in Mark Jeurgensmeier, *Religion as Social Vision: The Movement Against Untouchabilility in 20th Century Punjab* (Berkeley: University of California Press, 1982), p. 296.

7. E.M.S. Namboodiripad, *A History of the Indian Freedom Movement* (Trivandrum: Social Scientist Press, 1986), p. 492.

NOTES TO CHAPTER 6

1. From "Revolution and Counter-Revolution in Ancient India," *Dr. Babasaheb Ambedkar: Writings and Speeches, Volume 3* (Bombay: Government of Maharashtra, 1987), p. 275.

2. Untitled poem by Kamalsingh Baliram Ramteke in *Janata*, June 21, 1941.

3. *Ibid.*, January 15, 1938.

4. Ambedkar, *Revolution and Counter-Revolution*, p. 419.

5. Ambedkar, "Annihilation of Caste" in *Writings and Speeches, Volume 1*, p. 49.

6. Ambedkar, *Revolution and Counter-Revolution*, pp. 316-17.

7. *Ibid.*, p. 336.

8. Ambedkar, "Annihilation of Caste," p. 47.

9. *Ibid.*, p. 75-77.

10. Ambedkar, *Revolution and Counter-Revolution*, p. 336.

NOTES TO CHAPTER 7

1. The classic study is Eugene Irschick, *Politics and Social Conflict in South India* (Berkeley: University of California Press, 1969). For a recent discussion of the period of the Tamil non-brahman movement and the issues involved, see V.Geetha and S.V. Rajadurai, "NeoBrahmanism: An Intentional Fallacy?" *Economic and Political Weekly*, January 16-23, 1993.

2. See K. Murugesan and C. Subramanyam, *Singaravelu, First*

Communist in South India (New Delhi: Peoples' Publishing House, 1975), p. 64.

3. Quoted in Irschick, *Tamil Revivalism in the 1930s* (Madras, Cre-A, 1986), p. 224-25.
4. On Singaravelu, see Murugesan and Subramanysm, *op. cit.*
5. *Ibid.*, p. 83.
6. Sumit Sarkar, *Modern India, 1885-1947* (Delhi: Macmillan India Ltd., 1983), p. 351.
7. Anita Diehl, *Periyar E.V. Ramaswami* (Bombay: B.I. Publications, 1977), p. 62.
8. R.J. Moore, "Jinnah and the Pakistan Demand," in Robin Jeffrey, *et al*, ed., *India, Rebellion to Republic* (New Delhi: Sterling Publishers Pvt. Ltd., 1990).
9. Cited in Girin Phukon, "Ethnic Nationalism in North-East India: A Brief Overview of its Legacy," in Deka, *North-East Quarterly* 2:3, 1986.
10. Sarkar, *Modern India*, p. 378-80.
11. Diehl, *Periyar*, pp. 62-63.
12. *Ibid.*, p. 63.

NOTES TO CHAPTER 8

1. Asim Roy, "The High Politics of India's Partition: The Revisionist Perspective (Review Articles) in *Modern Asian Studies*, 24, 2, May 1991.
2. Jawaharlal Nehru, *Towards Freedom*, pp. 274-75.
3. From *Hind Swaraj*, in Raghavan Iyer, ed., *The Moral and Political Writings of Mahatma Gandhi, Volume I* (Oxford: Clarendon Press, 1986), p. 257.
4. *The Challenge to the South: Report of the South Commission* (New Delhi: Oxford University Press, 1992), pp. 84-85; see also IBRD, *The World Development Report, 1992* (New Delhi: World Bank, 1992), Table 1, pp. 218-19.
5. Estimate from Deepak Lal, *The Hindu Equilibrium, I: Cultural Stability and Economic Stagnation, India c.1500 BC-AD 1980* (London: Oxford University Press, 1988), p. 221.
6. Census of India, 1991; and *World Development Report, 1992*, Table 2.

7. *World Development Report, 1992*, Table 28, pp. 273-74 and Table 32, pp. 280-81.
8. *Hunger 1992: Second Annual Report on the State of World Hunger* (Washington, D.C.: Bread for the World Institute, 1992), Tables 2 and 3, pp. 180-83.
9. *World Development Report, 1990: Poverty*, p. 31.
10. Lal, *The Hindu Equilibrium*, p. 272.
11. B.P.R. Vithal, "Roots of Hindu Fundamentalism," *Economic and Political Weekly*, February 20-27, 1993.
12. M. Shivaiah, "Behind Hindu Growth Rate," *Economic and Political Weekly*, April 3, 1993.

NOTES TO CHAPTER 9

1. Dalit Panther Manifesto, in Barbara Joshi, *Untouchable! Voices of Dalit Liberation* (London: Zed Books, 1984), pp. 141-46.
2. Namdev Dhasal, "So That my Mother May be Convinced," translated by Jayant Karve, Vidyut Bhagwat, and Eleanor Zelliot, in Mulk Raj Anand and Eleanor Zelliot, *An Anthology of Dalit Literature* (New Delhi: Gyan Publishing House, 1992) p. 60-67
3. Keshav Meshram, *Ibid.*, p. 117.
4. Untitled Poem by Waman Nimbalkar, (called Just Poem) tr. Graham Smith, *Vagartha* 12, January 1976.
5. A.K. Roy, *The New Dalit Revolution* (1980), pp. 4, 10, 18.

NOTES TO CHAPTER 10

1. Waharu Sonavane, *Presidential Speech*, 5th Adivasi Sahitya Sammelan, Palghar, Mahrashtra, 23 December 1990 (translated from Marathi). Originally published in Marathi for the Adivasi Sahitya Sammelan by Sanjay Pethe. English translation by Gail Omvedt.
2. Madhav Gadgil and Ramchandra Guha, *This Fissured Land: An Ecological History of India* (New Delhi: Oxford University Press, 1992), pp.91—110.

3. Vandana Shiva, *Staying Alive: Women and Ecology in India* (New Delhi: Kali for Women Press, 1989).
4. *Time,* January 25, 1993.
5. Baburao Bagul, "Dalit Literature is but Human Literature" in Arjun Dangle, ed. *Poisoned Bread: Translations from Modern Marathi Dalit Literature,* Orient Longman 1992, pp. 283, 288.
6. *Ibid., pp.* 284—85.

NOTES TO CHAPTER 11

1. *Economist,* February 6, 1993, p. 21.
2. See Bharat Patankar, *Hindu ka Sindhu* (Marathi; Pune: Sugawa Prakashan, 1993); a shortened English version, "Hindu or Sindhu," *Frontier,* February 27, 1993.
3. Bagul, "Dalit Literature is But Human Literature," pp. 123-26.
4. Shashikant Hingonekar, "Ekalavya," *Asmitadarsh,* April/May/June 1989; translated by Gail Omvedt and Bharat Patankar.
5. Bagul, "You Who Have Made the Mistake", in Dangle (ed.) *Poisoned Bread,* p. 70; translated by Vilas Sarang.
6. Kishwar, in *Times of India,* January 28, 1993.
7. See J.M. Cadet, *Ramakien: The Stone Rubbings of the Thai Epic* (Bangkok: Kodansha International, 1970), p. 242.
8. Waman Kaidak "The Darkness within Me", in Anand and Zelliot, *Anthology,* p. 95.